Cambridge Elements

Elements in Language, Gender and Sexuality
edited by
Helen Sauntson
York St John University

DISCOURSE AND QUEER SINOPHONE MALE IDENTITIES

A Western Immigrant Perspective

Phil Freestone
The Hong Kong University of Science and Technology

Shaftesbury Road, Cambridge CB2 8EA, United Kingdom

One Liberty Plaza, 20th Floor, New York, NY 10006, USA

477 Williamstown Road, Port Melbourne, VIC 3207, Australia

314–321, 3rd Floor, Plot 3, Splendor Forum, Jasola District Centre, New Delhi – 110025, India

103 Penang Road, #05–06/07, Visioncrest Commercial, Singapore 238467

Cambridge University Press is part of Cambridge University Press & Assessment, a department of the University of Cambridge.

We share the University's mission to contribute to society through the pursuit of education, learning and research at the highest international levels of excellence.

www.cambridge.org
Information on this title: www.cambridge.org/9781009578646

DOI: 10.1017/9781009221269

© Phil Freestone 2025

This publication is in copyright. Subject to statutory exception and to the provisions of relevant collective licensing agreements, no reproduction of any part may take place without the written permission of Cambridge University Press & Assessment.

When citing this work, please include a reference to the DOI 10.1017/9781009221269

First published 2025

A catalogue record for this publication is available from the British Library

ISBN 978-1-009-57864-6 Hardback
ISBN 978-1-009-22124-5 Paperback
ISSN 2634-8772 (online)
ISSN 2634-8764 (print)

Cambridge University Press & Assessment has no responsibility for the persistence or accuracy of URLs for external or third-party internet websites referred to in this publication and does not guarantee that any content on such websites is, or will remain, accurate or appropriate.

For EU product safety concerns, contact us at Calle de José Abascal, 56, 1°, 28003 Madrid, Spain, or email eugpsr@cambridge.org

Discourse and Queer Sinophone Male Identities

A Western Immigrant Perspective

Elements in Language, Gender and Sexuality

DOI: 10.1017/9781009221269
First published online: October 2025

Phil Freestone
The Hong Kong University of Science and Technology
Author for correspondence: Phil Freestone, drphilfreestone@gmail.com

Abstract: This Element analyses the sociolinguistic navigation of cultural and ideological influence among queer male-identified individuals in Chengdu and Taipei. By analysing how queer and ethnically Chinese-identified individuals navigate ideological influences, it investigates some of the complexities of culture and identity and their dependence on semiotics and situated communication. Thus, the social affordances and constraints relevant to specific individuals in these contexts are described not only in terms of influences like 'Chinese culture' or 'Western ideology', but also in terms of the ongoing communicative processes through which they orient themselves to diverse structural influences. As such, this Element engages with the diversity typically subsumed into common identity categories. In turn, through its qualified deconstructionist approach to identity, it sheds novel light on the ideological complexity that tends to underlie queer individuals' performance of 'who they are' in Sinophone contexts and elsewhere.

Keywords: queer, Chinese, language, culture, discourse

© Phil Freestone 2025

ISBNs: 9781009578646 (HB), 9781009221245 (PB), 9781009221269 (OC)
ISSNs: 2634-8772 (online), 2634-8764 (print)

Contents

1 Introduction 1

2 Sociopolitical Influence in Queer Mainland China and Taiwan 4

3 Theoretical and Methodological Frameworks: Identity, Discourse and Positioning 15

4 Language and Queer Sinophone Identity Work in Taipei and Chengdu 22

5 Discussion 44

6 Conclusion 47

Appendices 48

References 52

1 Introduction

This Element analyses the sociolinguistic navigation of cultural and ideological influence among queer male-identified individuals in Chengdu and Taipei. Situated within the broader field of queer linguistics, it addresses what Cashman (2019: 521) identifies as the 'great need for a broader and more inclusive understanding of the diversity of LGBTQ expression and for further research in non-Anglo, non-English speaking communities'. In addition, it draws on queer Sinophone work which problematises the broad cultural schema prevalent in analysis of sexual minority lives in the region (Chiang and Heinrich, 2013; Chiang and Wong, 2020).[1] Building on these insights, I demonstrate how not all queer individuals in Sinophone contexts navigate the same sets of ideological influences, nor in the same ways, despite the widely presumed generalisability of 'Chinese gay' lives, and the ostensible stability of associated cultural and sexual labels. As Martin (2014: 41) acknowledges: 'The starting point for approaching contemporary Chinese cultures is acknowledgment of their difference, multiplicity, and fragmentation, but we should recognise, too, that new forms of shared experience are also enabled as a result of transnational flows of media and migration in a contemporary globalising world.'

It is this balance between cultural commonality and social diversity that this Element seeks to address. How can we recognise the diversity of lived realities amongst queer-identified people in Taiwan, mainland China[2] and other Sinophone contexts, while not losing sight of the very real social forces arising from an ostensibly tangible 'Chinese culture'? In a significant proportion of related work on queer lives, this difference and multiplicity tends to be subsumed into broad depictions of queer life in one or more Sinophone context(s). These are often accompanied by a problematic analytical dichotomy of 'Chinese vs Western' approaches to queer identities and queer politics, even in work which itself sets out to call for recognition of diversity under broad cultural and sexual labels (see Section 5).

In contrast, I analyse queer identity performance with a view to striking the balance between overgeneralisation and excessive deconstruction. I recognise that notions of 'Chinese culture' are often drawn upon as tools of identity work and that related cultural forces and social norms do shape shared practices

---

[1] Although the term *Sinophone* has previously been used to refer only to geographically marginal contexts (Shih, 2007), I use it for all people and communities who consider themselves as Chinese, howsoever defined.

[2] I use this term to navigate the sensitive issue of national and ethnic identity. I acknowledge that citizens of the People's Republic of China (PRC) tend to consider Taiwan one of its provinces, but my approach to identity means that individuals' articulations of identity must also be understood in their own terms. My discussion employs the terms that participants use to describe themselves. I take a neutral stance on geopolitics related to Taiwan.

across Sinophone societies. I also recognise that there are tangible differences between these societies, in terms of salient trends in social practice. However, I also note that associated life stories are highly diverse, both within and across communities delimited in national, ethnic and regional terms. I therefore focus on the personalised navigation of distinct ideological, sociocultural and sociopolitical influences in individual cases. In this way, I also build on the important work of Chun (2017: x) in aiming to 'transcend ... literal discussions of Chineseness and situate them within their respective historical contexts and underlying geopolitical formative processes [and] to problematize Chineseness as constitutive of an ongoing historical framework [and] to problematize the nature of contexts that invoke Chineseness as an ethnic or cultural problem'.

The novel contribution of my approach, however, is to draw on the field of queer linguistics by focusing on the role of language in identity work and on the emergent communicative processes through which individuals navigate diverse structural influences. Thus, I start from a 'scepticism towards categories and, more specifically, identity categories, criticising the way they may cause ignorance of intra-categorical heterogeneity, exclusion, marginalisation of less prototypical category members, and a stigmatisation of non-conforming practices' (Motschenbacher, 2020: 2–3). However, this does not mean entirely dissolving broad everyday categories like *gay* and *Chinese* by becoming lost in the somewhat ephemeral deconstruction which is considered typical of classic postmodernist philosophers (see De Fina, Schiffrin and Bamberg, 2006). Indeed, I take the sociopolitical weight and emic significance of such categories seriously and remain wary of the 'frenzied postmodernist pursuit of difference, deconstruction and ambiguity' (Forrest, 1994: 99). For example, I recognise the importance of notions of culture to individuals' senses of everyday belonging and to their performance of queer identity.

Similarly, as will become clear in what follows, I recognise the ideological power of wealthy Western countries in sustaining Global 'North' and 'South' inequalities, as well as the powerful globalised reach of capitalist models of queer identity which have their roots in Western centres of power. As such, I acknowledge that there is indeed some degree of utility in thinking in terms of broad 'identities', especially when it comes to understanding individuals' senses of self, and/or issues of racism, decolonisation and global social justice. Furthermore, I build on the body of work which deconstructs blinkered and Eurocentric narratives of linear 'West to rest' development of queer identity (e.g. Oswin, 2006; Rofel, 2007), as well as on problematisations of the postcolonial viewpoints which have led to an under-representation of regional diversity in the Sinophone sphere, and Asia more broadly (e.g. Chiang and Heinrich, 2013). Concurrently, I actively recognise how everyday power dynamics in postcolonial contexts are always inflected by history and I therefore reflect carefully on my positionality and privilege as a white British researcher from a country with a highly problematic colonial past.

On a theoretical level, this Element also contributes to ongoing discussions on the analytical value and/or limitations of 'queering' common identity categories, drawing on the *qualified deconstructionist* perspective taken up in my previous related work (Freestone, 2023, 2024). In this way, I provide a novel, discourse analytic point of view on the ideological complexity which tends to underlie individuals' performance of 'who they are' – that is, their *identity work*. Identity is therefore seen herein as significantly dependent on semiotics and as fluid *and* stable (see Section 3). Of course, this is not a new theoretical position, since it emerges from classic post-structuralist philosophy like that of Foucault (1972, 1978) and is also very well established in fields such as discourse analysis (such as in the work of Jones, 2016) and queer linguistics (such as in the work of Motschenbacher, 2011, 2021 and Motschenbacher and Stegu, 2013). However, the sociocultural approach to discourse analysis I take up (Blommaert, 2005; Jones, 2016), is somewhat novel in its operationalisation of the interplay between language, culture and ideology. This approach insists on a foregrounding of the role of everyday communication in the production and reproduction of hegemonic discourse systems.

For example, in the case of queer individuals in Sinophone contexts, this cultural and ideological influence can sometimes be understood in terms of the situated, sociolinguistic appropriation of *discourse systems* such as the Confucian and the utilitarian. These systems entail *interpretive frameworks* of assumptions, categories, logics, claims, norms, ethics and values influencing speech and actions in a given communicative situation (Scollon et al, 2012). Importantly, because the influence of these frameworks is traceable in speech in situated communication, language is seen as central to their articulation and reproduction. From this perspective, ostensibly stable 'identities' are seen as multiple, emergent, individualised and situationally contingent. Concurrently, notions of cultural belonging are seen as relevant as and when they are drawn upon or, perhaps, resisted or remoulded by specific individuals. This allows for a recognition of the social diversity within associated communities and also of the fact that identity work varies significantly across specific moments of communication and across any one individual's lifetime. It also allows for a recognition of the fact that identity work always depends partly on embodied semiotics such as a style of walking or dressing, which can add extra nuance to the complexity of performed selves. However, the focus herein is specifically on the sociolinguistic level.

In sum, the first key aim of this Element is to contribute to the field of queer linguistics by applying a discourse analytic and sociolinguistic approach to identity in Sinophone sexual minority communities. Its international relevance comes through its use of two 'similar yet distinct' sociopolitical and sociocultural contexts to interrogate the sometimes paradoxical processes of queer identity work which take place both within them and across the globe. In fact, due to the historical specificities of the core Sinophone region, which has led to the unique characteristics of Taiwan and mainland China respectively, I argue that the cases of the men I engaged with are especially useful for uncovering the complexity underlying the identity terms taken for granted every day and everywhere (like *Chinese* and *Asian* but also *Western* and *gay*). The second key aim is to offer a relatively novel methodological and theoretical perspective to the existing body of work on queer lives in mainland China and Taiwan. I propose that queer practice within and across these Sinophone contexts entails much more than simple choices between the spuriously dichotomous 'Chinese'/'Western' lifestyles, or between queer political orientations taken to correspond to other broad ethnic, national or regional distinctions. Thus associated notions of broadly delimited cultural influence are problematised (but not dismissed) and cultural and ideological influence is instead analysed with keen attention to the partly fluid nature of identity work as it emerges in specific moments of communication. With all this in mind, the research questions I will be addressing are as follows:

1. What does the language of queer male-identified individuals in Chengdu and Taipei suggest regarding the role of various discourse systems in identity work?
2. What does the positioning of these individuals vis-à-vis such discourse systems reveal about their navigation of globalised and localised sociopolitical and cultural influences?
3. To what extent are ostensibly stable notions of culture, ethnicity and sexuality useful and accurate in analysing queer identities in Sinophone contexts?

2 Sociopolitical Influence in Queer Mainland China and Taiwan

2.1 Qualified Deconstructionism and Queer Sinophone Identities

This is not the first study which deals with queer issues in Taiwan and mainland China respectively (see Kong, 2023; Liu, 2015; Liu and Rofel, 2010). As noted, however, it does so from a relatively novel theoretical perspective on queer Sinophone lives. This approach is described in detail in Section 3, but its key implication is to acknowledge, but not to overgeneralise, the everyday articulations of ethnic Chinese identity that are commonly shared between mainland

China and Taiwan. Despite clear social trends related to locally specific political and cultural realities (e.g. same-gender marriage is legal in Taiwan but not in mainland China), it would be a mistake to imply that the only pertinent structural influences on contemporary youth in each place are those which are necessarily localised. After all, the ethnically Han Chinese majority in Taiwan has its geographical origins in early modern China and related cultural roots tend to influence trends in social practice. Thus, while queer lives in Sinophone contexts cannot be accurately delimited only according to broad geographical and/or cultural boundaries, and ostensibly widespread social trends are not always universal in their implications for a given life story, I nevertheless acknowledge that there *are* characteristically mainland Chinese and Taiwanese ways of 'being queer' through language and semiotics, at least to some extent.

My discussion on these themes builds upon previous work which engages with the complex similarities and differences in geopolitics, culture and queer life across Sinophone contexts, such as Kong's (2023) discussion of Taiwan and mainland China (along with Hong Kong), and Liu's (2015: 313) comparative analysis of the former two, which entails a careful balance between the 'anti-universalist impulse in Queer Theory' and the 'anti-essentialist argument [which] has rendered any indication of "Chinese difference" or "Chinese specificity" politically suspect'. With this in mind, the comparisons made in the following overview of sociopolitical trends, while admittedly somewhat dichotomous, are considered a necessary introduction of Taiwan and mainland China as distinct queer contexts. However, in later sections, I more fully apply a qualified deconstructionist point of view which, in this case, means understanding sociopolitical specificities not only in terms of relatively clear-cut regional distinctions, but also with keen attention to the inevitable variety and complexity of individuals responses, both within and across individual life stories.

Before discussing the two sociopolitical contexts in question, some points about my choice of terminology should be noted. Firstly, I refer to the individuals described in this Element as *queer male-identified*. The choice to use *male-identified*, as opposed to *male* or *man*, arises from my post-structuralist preference for considering identity in terms of identification, which I describe in Section 3. Meanwhile, using *queer* allows me to avoid seemingly innocuous but in fact potentially problematic alternatives such as the following:

(a) *Gay* has the potential to be heavily socioculturally loaded. That is, the fact that this is an English term can have important implications in terms of identity (see e.g. Bao, 2018; Ho, 2010).

(b) *MSM* (men who have sex with men) and other medicalised terms connote sexual activity rather than felt attraction. The focus herein is on how individuals articulate their understanding of sexual self and other, as opposed to their actual sexual practice, because these two things may not necessarily be aligned (see Boellstorff 2011).
(c) *Tongzhi*.³ Although this has been the most popular Mandarin equivalent to *gay* or *queer*, this not usually a term with which the men I engaged usually identified. This term is also socioculturally loaded, both as a Mandarin term and as a term with an overtly communist mainland Chinese history.
(d) *Homosexual* and other terms which foreground (biological) sex over (psychosocial) gender and/or have come to be widely associated with negative, pathological connotations (cf. the close Mandarin correlate *tongxinglian*).

In contrast to these terms, the label *queer* allows for a fuller acknowledgement of the diversity of emic understandings and modes of performing sexual identity often subsumed into terms like *gay* and *tongzhi*. Thus my choice of terminology helps in exposing the problematic nature of assuming, based on a given category, that an individual's lifestyle and identity work follow a presumed self-evident path. In previous work, I have used other terminology such as *same-gender-attracted* on the basis that *queer* can also be a loaded term due to its political connotations (Freestone, 2023, 2024). However, to avoid unwieldy terminology in this Element, I do not use it herein to refer to a consciously adopted 'queer' identity. Although I certainly recognise the potential importance of such identity work, I have opted to use *queer* not to connote a politicised identity position in itself, but only to refer to an emic articulation of self against the grain of societal norms. That is, queer refers herein only to a positioning of self as different from the mainstream in terms of sexuality, however this might be conceived by the person in question.

2.2 Mainland China

Contrary to certain narratives which are prominent outside the region, the queer community in China is not helpless in its struggle against stigma, nor is it entirely at the mercy of authoritarian social pressure (see Song, 2021). Indeed, it is important to recognise, as key author Hongwei Bao (2020: 3–4) does, that:

---

³ *Comrade* (lit. 'same will/same spirit') is the most common identity term for Sinophone sexual minority identity since the 1990s, with an ideologically loaded semantic field with potential connotations related to ethnicity (Chinese vs other), politics (communist vs other) and modernity (1980s and 1990s vs today) (see Wong, 2005a, 2005b, 2008a, 2008b).

Western media are often full of reports about China's lack of human rights, or sexual minorities' suffering in the PRC from a heteronormative society and an authoritarian government. All these reports are likely to be true, but a narrow focus on the political system and human rights misses the point about what is happening on the ground, in the communities and in people's everyday lives.

For example, I perceived a widespread sense of acceptance and tolerance of queerness amongst the relatively young, urban and educated communities I worked in as a university teacher (albeit mainly in highly ranked institutions with relatively cosmopolitan students). Similarly, Wang and Ma (2020) found that the university students they surveyed tended to be generally supportive in their attitudes to queer communities. In fact, I believe that anyone who engages extensively with the queer community in mainland China, especially in relatively developed cities and/or relatively privileged social contexts, is likely to note a significant number of lives shared between queer partners which are largely uninterrupted by broader social and political constraints. Indeed, many such individuals have stable relationships and enjoy acceptance of their sexual minority identity amongst friends, and sometimes amongst family. This reflects what has been a significant overall increase in public and official tolerance of queerness in mainland China over the past thirty years, despite recent setbacks (Engebretsen, 2014; Jeffreys and Yu, 2015). Some key related historical events were the 2001 removal of *tongxinglian* (homosexuality) from the list of mental disorders of the Chinese Psychiatry Association (classified as such in 1978) and the 1997 abolition of the crime of hooliganism through which queer men were often harassed and prosecuted as *liumang* (hooligans). Widespread changes in salient conceptions of the family have also emerged which have had important implications for the queer community. For example, the taken-for-granted desirability of the traditional heteronormative family unit (a man and a woman married, with children) has been challenged in many ways due to factors such as modernisation and ideological shifts amongst contemporary youth (Davis, 2014; Wei, 2021).

However, despite these broadly progressive aspects of social context, and despite the continuing need to correct the prevalence of related short-sighted views from outside mainland China, describing sexual minority life there in overly positive terms risks overlooking the significant social struggles that many queer-identified individuals still face. This is especially true when all regions and all social strata of mainland China are considered. Similarly, being overly focused on empowerment and individual agency means risking overlooking the continuing widespread and pernicious impact of normativity, homophobia and repressive institutions on mainland Chinese queers (Song, 2021). On a broader level, for example, widespread negativity remains around queer sexualities amongst the general public, as noted in a relatively recent quantitative study in which Xie and Peng (2018) found that 78.53 per cent of their sample (based on national census statistics) believed same-sex sexual behaviour is always wrong. Similarly, a major United Nations report found that 68.5 per cent of respondents in relatively modern and cosmopolitan cities in mainland China 'could not accept homosexuality' (UNDP and USAID, 2014). Of course, this study was published over a decade ago and, furthermore, such generalised statistics may not offer accurate representations of opinion amongst the vast range of relevant ethnic, class-based, racial and regional economic realities, but they nevertheless help in sketching general societal trends.

It should also be noted that various other significant factors indicate a general lack of tolerance of queerness in mainland China. For example, Liu (2021) found that 'gays' were framed in social media posts in terms of (1) political misconduct in opposition to public opinion, (2) a political movement to promote 'Westernization' and 'independence' and/or (3) a direct path to immorality and self-destruction. More pernicious forms of stigmatisation also remain common. For example, Zheng's (2015: 47–54) study of online content found a high prevalence of 'extreme, aggressive and sometimes violently anti-gay' attitudes. Furthermore, it is not uncommon to see queer-identified individuals framed as a threat to the national and cultural integrity of 'we Chinese', or as enemies of traditional values. For example, effeminate men are frequently framed as a threat to national stability, as reflected in the discursively powerful and institutionally sanctioned notion of a crisis of masculinity (Zheng, 2015), which puts significant pressure on men, and especially youth, to act in conventionally masculine ways. As in other locations around the world, this type of hegemonic masculine narrative can be seriously oppressive, and not least for those who tend to act in ways generally considered relatively effeminate.

In addition, it is socially significant that traditionalist and pernicious associations with HIV/AIDS also remain widespread (Zheng, 2015). For example, although Wang and Ma (2020) found that mainland Chinese English-language newspapers' representations of LGBTQ+ people were relatively progressive overall, they also noted that associations with HIV/AIDS still characterised their reports. These stigmatising conceptions often also correspond to hegemonic narratives of *public order*, *goodness* and *customs* and to the associated construal of *immoral*, *unstable* and/or *perverted* 'others'. Interestingly, this corresponds to similar conceptions in Taiwan of offences against virtuous customs (*shanliang fengsu*) or activities entailing obscene conduct (*weixie xingwei*), although the prominence of these narratives has faded much more there than in mainland China. However, we should remember that these ideas were nevertheless widely and sometimes brutally influential in relatively recent periods of history in Taiwan too.

Another important factor is that mainland China's centralised and heavily censored media system strongly discourages expression of non-normative sexual identity (Chang and Ren, 2017; Zheng, 2015). This means that positive role models or empowering depictions of non-normative love experiences are very rare, extremely subtle or entirely absent. In fact, the State Administration of Press, Publication, Radio, Film and Television relatively recently made a decisive ruling which stated that non-heterosexual relations were 'abnormal', categorising them along with incest, perversion, sexual abuse and violence (Shaw and Zhang, 2018). The effects of such a policy are undoubtedly tangible – for example, in terms of reducing the potentially liberating kinds of queer visibility and queer role models in popular culture for young people coming to terms with being sexually different. In addition, mainland China's education system and mainstream print media routinely construe queer identity as a social problem and/or in terms of 'abnormal' sexual desires, 'confused' or 'sensitive' individuals and unfortunate individual childhood circumstances (Chang and Ren, 2017).

The drama series *Addicted* (*Shang Yin*), released in 2016, was a poignant example of the associated complexity of queer representation in mainland Chinese media. This was a high-school story focused on the romantic relationship of two male characters which went viral inside and outside the queer community but was subsequently removed by censors, generating widespread discussion in online news and on social media (Ellis-Petersen, 2016; Song, 2021; Yan, 2016). This reflected the now classic ambiguity surrounding the online presence of such material and the careful moral negotiation that tends to inform and constrain mainstream popular culture production. Another example is *Coming Home* (*Huijia*), a perceptive and moving short video released by PFLAG China, a popular family-focused queer NGO. This video touches on issues of family, normativity and sexual orientation by broaching the typically challenging issue of a queer individual going to the family home for the spring festival and facing the problematic interaction of their queer identification with their family relationships. This video also went viral, reportedly having 250 million online views before being taken offline relatively quickly (Huang and Brouwer, 2018). These examples reflect the cat-and-mouse game between censors and queer media producers, which seems to be continuing apace at the time of writing. Also relevant is the more recent active restriction of non-normative media content and the concurrent 'cancelling' on key social media platforms of celebrities who are part of the queer community. Indeed, what well-established mainland-China-based LGBTQ+ scholar Wei Wei (2018: 9) argues still seems true: that 'many insightful observers of Chinese society have noted its turn to greater conservatism in recent years'.

Also relevant here is mainland China's infamous and sophisticated system of information monitoring, censorship and internet control and its powerful ideological effects (Chen and Ang, 2011; Esarey and Xiao, 2011; King et al., Pan and Roberts, 2013). However, the role of the internet in queer mainland China should certainly not be conceived in entirely negative terms. For example, the dramatic rise in internet access beginning in the 1990s was crucial in facilitating increased awareness of queer lives (Kam, 2013; Rofel, 2007; Wei, 2007). This was especially true in the early days of widespread internet access, when there was a notable proliferation of queer-related websites and web-based tools (Berry et al., 2003; Cao and Lu, 2014; Ho, 2010). More recently, dating apps like Blued and Finka (formerly called Aloha) have played a similarly central role as queer social platforms and this seems to reflect a relative tolerance of queerness on a broader societal level compared with earlier decades. As well as the articulation of queer identity and belonging that these technologies facilitate, they can be especially socially important, considering the relative lack of clubs, societies and other queer-friendly spaces/groups. In a similar way, exploration through online pornography has also been analysed as key to developing 'sexual literacy' and queer identity in a context of scarce access to public information and queer social engagement. However, on a critical level, it should also perhaps be noted that these issues pertain to complex questions of class, access to resources (Ding and Song, 2023).

Another aspect of sociopolitical context which is relevant here is the widespread trend for self-censorship amongst authors, journalists and academics who write on related topics in mainland China (see Ho et al., 2018; Kong, 2019; Wei, 2018; Yang, 2019; Yuen, 2015). For example, there is significant stigmatisation in the field of academic publishing of topics deemed 'sensitive' (*mingan*), a somewhat fluid notion which appears to pertain to anything diverging from that which is broadly perceived as 'normal'. Importantly also, all organised public protest remains illegal in mainland China, and, during the Xi Jinping era, there has been an increasing governmental focus on preventing uprisings and challenges to the current legal and political structure (Yang, 2019: 662). This should, of course, also be understood in the context of the great creativity and agency that defines queer resistance in the mainland and which has been described, for example, as nomadic or guerilla activism (Bao, 2018; Rofel, 2007) or in terms of playful, creative and resilient engagement with censorship (Ding and Song, 2023: 2470).

Clearly, the overall situation concerning the influence of societal attitudes and sociopolitical factors on individuals in mainland China is complex, if not paradoxical. Furthermore, the diversity of developmental, regional and urban–rural social realities across this vast country adds to this complexity. This has been partly illustrated in several book-length ethnographic studies documenting queer male communities in specific regions in mainland China and shedding some light on its huge regional and socioeconomic diversity (Cummings, 2022; Miller, 2023; Zheng, 2015). However, what Elisabeth Engebretsen (2014: 4) noted in her ethnographic project amongst the *lala* (female-identified queer) community in mid 2000s Beijing seems to remain broadly true across all regions and social strata: that in mainland China 'new freedoms and opportunities for social activism, leisure and intimacies' interact with 'strict political authority circumscribing liberating and progressive processes', with clear effects on everyday lives. Building on such insights, what follows in Section 4 is an investigation of contemporary cases which draws on my own ethnographic observations, and in which I pay keen attention to the diversity of individual life stories across the broader queer community.

2.3 Taiwan

Firstly, it should be noted that I spent considerably less time in Taiwan than in mainland China; I acknowledge the consequent limitations on my knowledge of the former social context. In fact, my choice to carry out research there was, in some sense, made on the grounds of triangulation, because I wanted to compare my experiences in mainland China, across a decade or so, with this culturally 'similar yet different' context. I discuss the background to these choices in greater detail in Section 3. Despite these limitations, however, it was abundantly clear to me that there were palpable social and cultural differences between the two sites when it came to queer identity performance and queer identity politics. For example, the queer community in Taiwan is significantly more publicly visible than that in mainland China, and related social issues tend to be much more publicly prominent, for example, in mainstream media and state education. However, it should also be noted that many pertinent sociopolitical changes in Taiwan only emerged in the early 2000s, reflecting the ending of fifty-five years of continuous rule by the repressive, right-wing Kuomintang government. This made way for the Democratic Progressive Party (DPP), which has been focused on pluralist policies and liberalisation (Damm, 2005). Also, the considerable economic development of the 1980s and 1990s made Taiwan an 'Asian Tiger' economy, leading to key related social factors such as increased potential freedom from the family for many young people.

Importantly, this occurred at a much earlier stage in history than in mainland China.

It is also important to note that, in the 1970s and 1980s, the queer community in Taiwan, like that of mainland China, was still made up of 'discrete subcultures largely invisible to the general public' (Berry et al., 2003: 90). What makes the two places distinct in this regard, however, is the highly visible and infuential civil–political queer emancipation movement which emerged in 1990s Taiwan (Berry et al., 2003: 90). For example, numerous queer community groups, university student organisations and recognised research groups formed which became part of an impactful, broader campaign focused on recognition and equality (Lee, 2016; Martin, 2014). It is significant that Taiwan's first openly lesbian social group was formed in 1990, that the first public queer-related human rights hearing was held in 1993, and that both the first public queer rights demonstration and the first application for same-sex marriage happened in 1995. Around this time also, some key literary and popular culture figures were publicly open about their same-gender attraction. Also, various scholars published well-received work calling for more tolerance of sexual minorities and demonstrating that homosexuality was not pathological, but simply a sexual preference (Erni and Spires, 2001; Huang, 2011), and key public social groups, online chatrooms (BBS boards) and community magazines also contributed significantly to the LGBTQ+ movement (Erni and Spires, 2001; Jackson et al., 2008; Tan, 2001).

These shifts in Taiwanese society were also reflected on the level of popular culture, with various successful queer-themed novels and films released, including the novel *Crystal Boys* (*Neizi* [lit. 'bad sons']) (1983) by Pai Hsien-Yung.[4] This novel is widely cited as the first novel in Chinese which deals with central (rather than implicit) queer themes and is therefore acclaimed as a significant landmark in the public recognition of the queer community across the Sinophone sphere (Liu, 2010; Martin, 2003). Similarly, the 1993 release of Ang Lee's acclaimed film *The Wedding Banquet* was also a key moment for Taiwan's queer community. This film was loosely based on another key novel of the 1980s: *Paper Marriage* (*Zhihun*) by Chen Ruoxi, a story of a woman from mainland China who marries an American gay man in order to move to the USA. She then falls in love with him in the final stage of his life before he dies of AIDS. Liu (2010, 2015) describes this novel as a pivotal critique of heteronormative marriage expectations and citizenship.

These examples reflect the significant changes in public perceptions of LGBTQ+ issues, and the contrast with mainland China is poignantly clear.

---

[4] English translation published in 1989.

Indeed, although we must acknowledge the work of mainland activists (see Bao, 2018) and the impactful groundwork of academic pioneers like Li Yinhe and Zhang (1994) (and activists like Wan Yanhai), the reach and sociopolitical impact of similar work in Taiwan was undeniably much greater. In turn, this has ultimately led to a social atmosphere that many locals and visitors consider to be one of the most progressive in Asia, surrounding queer issues (Hsu and Yen, 2017; Huang, 2011). This reputation for tolerance was also significantly bolstered by the 2017 high court recognition of same-sex marriage, which was overtly supported by the president, Tsai Ing-wen (Agerholm, 2017; Haas, 2017). Sociopolitical differences between the two sites in question are also clearly reflected in the relative visibility of queer subcultures in public spaces, such as in the proliferation of queer venues in Taiwan since the late 1980s. The situation in Taipei has led to the development of what is now a highly active and visible LGBTQ+ café and park culture in Taipei's Ximending, close to 'February 28th Memorial Park' (formerly 'New Park'). Interestingly, this park was an important location in the story the novel *Crystal Boys*, confirming its iconic status in local queer history.

Furthermore, this history was described in detail on a large, rainbow-coloured information board placed prominently in the centre of 'February 28th Memorial Park', Taipei. Although only one example of what might be considered pertinent *linguistic landscapes* (Landry and Bourhis, 1997), the presence of this board in a city-centre park was representative, for me, of a strikingly different level of overtly queer public artefacts in Taiwan and mainland China respectively. For me, this reflects one key contrast between the two sites in contemporary times: the general level of institutional and public acknowledgement of the queer community and its history. For example, although there is not space to reproduce them all here, I took many photographs of rainbow flags, LGBTQ+-oriented posters and billboards and openly LGBTQ+ venues in Taiwanese urban centres. I also collected many related leaflets and flyers which were publicly available and unambiguously queer. This contrasted sharply with what I was able to note, collect and photograph in mainland China over the years. On this theme, it is also notable that one of the crosswalks near Ximending has also been painted in rainbow colours and become somewhat iconic on social media, which is one example of how the physical landscape of Taipei is very much distinct from that of major cities in mainland China in terms of state-sanctioned queer visibility. Furthermore, Taipei Pride is now a hugely popular annual international event, the biggest of its kind in Asia, while attempts to hold similar events in mainland China have been either unsuccessful or significantly hampered either by direct action by the police, or indirect pressure from authorities resulting in self-censorship. More broadly, it is also well documented that the broader mainland Chinese queer emancipation movement tends to respond to associated structural pressures in less overt and public ways (see e.g. Bao, 2018, 2020).

Despite the comparatively progressive[5] context of Taiwan described here, one notable stigmatising force is that of politically influential transnational Christian groups such as True Love Alliance and Alliance for the Protection of Family. Importantly, the social and political influence of such conservative groups is much less powerful in mainland China. Such organisations typically frame sexual minorities as unhealthy, promiscuous and/or a threat to social stability and the well-being of children (Cheng et al., 2016; Lee, 2016, 2017; Wang et al., 2009). It is also relevant that there is considerable wealth and political influence within the Christian community, although a very small section of Taiwanese society identifies as Christian (Cheng et al., 2016; Lee, 2017), as is also the case in Hong Kong (Kong, 2023). Furthermore, J. Ho (2010) suggests that direct cooperation between Christian groups and the state has allowed overtly anti-queer groups in Taiwan to gain significant political power.

In sum, although the events and trends discussed in this section should not be used as a basis for broad, generalised conclusions about the lived realities of all queer people in Taiwan or mainland China, they do show how the foundations laid from the 1970s onwards have led to distinct atmospheres in terms of social and political acceptance of queer people. Associated social affordances and constraints are undoubtedly relevant to queer individuals' choices in identity performance in both sites and, as such, a certain degree of generalisation can be justified. Indeed, the differences I observed between Taipei and Chengdu did seem to have clear implications for identity work amongst people like the men I engaged with. However, although analysis of identity and culture (sexual or otherwise) requires keen attention to potentially consequential historical and sociocultural factors like those discussed in this section, I nevertheless suggest that such factors should not lead researchers to overgeneralised conclusions about social practice and/or perceptions of cultural belonging across a given national, regional, ethnic, cultural or sexuality-based population. That is, I argue that we cannot assume that all queer lives and approaches to identity in Taiwan and mainland China are inevitably fundamentally different, despite the contrasts between the two societies discussed here.

---

[5] Although notions of 'Chinese socialism' in mainland China are also sometimes framed as 'progressive' based on implications that aspects of Marxist ideology are widely adopted by the activist community (Bao, 2018), I use the term differently here, to represent a political approach which aims directly for explicit and complete queer visibility and legal recognition of queer diversity. As the current discussion shows, this is not the path generally taken in mainland China.

In what follows, therefore, I consider social, legal and political factors like those discussed in this section alongside the variation I noted in semiotically mediated identity performance across related communities. This balanced approach is the foundation of the discursive and ethnographic perspective I offer, and which I will explain in detail in Section 3.

3 Theoretical and Methodological Frameworks: Identity, Discourse and Positioning

3.1 Queer Sinophone Identity as Performance

As noted above, seeing identity as a partly emergent process allows us to account for some of the social and cultural complexity underlying terms like 'Chinese' and 'Western'. This seems especially important in the case of the highly mediated and globalised social worlds of people like the relatively young, urban and educated megacity-urban individuals in this study (see section 3.3 for details). Indeed, the multifarious and diverse identity work which I found to emerge amongst them is useful in bringing the whole notion of identity, as it is commonly understood, into question. For example, despite strong tendencies for study participants in both Taiwan and mainland China to describe themselves as *gay* and *Chinese* (sometimes as an ethnicity, sometimes as a nationality and sometimes as both), my analysis of their identity work also showed how these notions interacted with other diverse aspects of belonging, and how this tended to seem important to their navigation of social and ideological contexts.

In investigating identity in the contexts in question, I therefore follow influential cultural studies scholars in understanding it as a process of *becoming* rather than *being*, and as featuring their intersecting *identifications* with various emically conceived communities that become relevant to their interactions (Hall and Du Gay, 1996). Such a perspective has also given rise to notions such as LePage and Tabouret-Keller's (1985) *acts of identity*, Butler's (1990) *performativity* and Goffmann's (1959) *performance of self in everyday life*, which also inform the *discursive-sociocultural* approach to language and identity that I adopt.[6] This perspective is not built upon a stand-alone framework, but a broad body of work which builds on foundational work in discourse analysis and focuses on the mutually constitutive interplay of language, ideology and identity in situated interactions (Blommaert, 2005; Gee, 2014 [1999]; Jones, 2016). I argue that this perspective is uniquely suited to tracing the use of linguistic and semiotic tools of identity performance in instances of language use which are often ostensibly banal. In the case of this study, it therefore allows

---

[6] An excellent overview of such work can be found, for example, in Block (2022).

for an especially clear elucidation of the fuzzy philosophical, political and cultural influences on individuals in the two cosmopolitan, urban Sinophone contexts in question.

Importantly, applying this theoretical point of view entails sacrificing the convenience of analytical generalisation. In line with this, while I am indebted to authors who sketch queer life in mainland China and Taiwan in broad terms, the novel contribution I propose is to build on this work by actively recognising diversity in related communities. As noted in the introduction, I therefore draw upon the notion of discourse systems (Scollon et al., 2012) in place of broad notions of culture and descriptions of practice delimited on the level of a whole society. This allows for an alternative understanding of identity based on individuals' emergent alignments with/distancings from associated 'ways of seeing the world' (Sunderland, 2004). These emerge through what they say and do, so speech and social action are seen here as entailing the navigation of the complex and overlapping frameworks of social, moral and ethical assumptions – that is, discourse systems which delimit and guide that individuals understand to be 'normal' and/or self-evidently 'good' or 'bad'. Thus, the appropriation of discourse systems can be seen in terms of the employment of *heteroglossic* 'voices' that have 'spoken' before in a given social context, and which have led to a degree of ideological sedimentation within the community in question (Bakhtin, 1986 [1979]). I will exemplify this in the context of project data in Section 4.

3.2 Identity as Positioning

Along with the notion of discourse systems, a key approach I use for deeper engagement with the complexity of sociolinguistic identity work is to view it in terms of *positioning*. The notion of positioning is a heuristic for charting the emic senses of belonging articulated in specific moments of communication (Block, 2022; Bucholtz and Hall, 2005; Davies and Harré, 1990), thus:

> Who one is ... is always an open question with a shifting answer depending upon the positions made available within one's own and others' discursive practices and within those practices, the stories through which we make sense of our own and others' lives. (Davies and Harré, 1990: 46)

For example, although an individual like me may identify (and 'feel') 'British' throughout their life and across diverse social situations, there will inevitably be moments in which they might be perceived to be 'being more British', based on the linguistic and other semiotic signals they gave off to others. These moments would inevitably be shaped, to some extent, by factors like the other people involved in the conversation, the place, the time and the specifics of the social situation. Also, the emergence of 'Britishness' in such a case would be a two-way process, with the identifications (i.e. senses of belonging) claimed being recognised and ratified to varying degrees by others (Gee, 2014 [1999]). Furthermore, although at some point in their life, such an individual may hypothetically become entirely 'un-British' – for example, in legal terms due to renouncing nationality – they would nevertheless still be able to 'be' British, at least to some extent, in various ways and at various times. From a discourse-analytic perspective in which scrutiny of language is prioritised, this corresponds to what Davies and Harré (1990: 47) refer to as the 'discursive production of a variety of selves ... conjured up during conversational interactions' – that is, the process of positioning.

More recently, De Fina (2013: 41) has critiqued Davies and Harré's assumption that 'positions automatically come with attached world views and philosophies' and their 'rather mechanical association between identities and sets of beliefs, lines of arguments and roles' (cf. De Fina and Georgakopoulou, 2012). Similarly, Block (2022) proposes a more nuanced model of positioning which he labels positioning theory. However, perhaps the most widely applied use of the notion is found in Bucholtz and Hall's (2004, 2005) framework for charting identity through close analysis of the linguistic and semiotic aspects of individuals' communication, which productively operationalises the notion of positioning (or *positionality*, in their terms). Although I do not employ all the specific terminology they put forward, I do build on their work in considering identity as 'in part an outcome of interactional negotiation and contestation, in part an outcome of others' perceptions and representations and in part an effect of larger ideological processes and material structures that may become relevant to interaction' (Bucholtz and Hall, 2005: 606).

With the associated intersectionality and fluidity of identity as a focal point, this Element also considers identity work in terms of the linguistic *resources* participants draw from their sociolinguistic *repertoires* in moments of situated communication (Blommaert, 2005). For example, rather than treating what study participants said as caused by and/or indicative of neatly generalisable cultural, sexual or other identities, I trace the ideological influences that leads them to speak about themselves and others in certain ways, in certain situations. Such linguistic acts exemplify their drawing resources from repertoires or, in other words, drawing words, sounds and gestures from their store of learned communicative tools. Crucially, I also see this in terms of their appropriation of discourse systems in any given moment of communication. However, this does not simply mean ascribing one discourse system to one instance of speech. For example, what some participants said to me as part of this project sometimes seemed to index the influence of various associated interpretive systems of taken-for-granted assumptions some of which could be seen as simultaneously local *and* globalised, modern *and* traditional, 'Eastern' *and* 'Western' and 'gay' *and* 'straight', amongst other things. In such a case, I might draw on notions such as the Confucian discourse system and the utilitarian discourse system to tease out some, but of course not all, of the relevant complexities of ideology and identity (Scollon et al., 2012). Although I do not claim that this approach is the be-all and end-all in terms of identity analysis, I do suggest that it allows us to think outside the usual box of broad societal and cultural sketches in analysis of social practice in queer Sinophone contexts.

3.3 Participants and Their 'Identities'

Participants in each location were recruited mainly through existing social links and friend-of-friend recommendations, but also sometimes through online and face-to-face social networks. In each case, I introduced myself as a friend first, then later invited those I thought might be interested in the project to take part. It should be noted that I did not set out to find a representative sample of any particular group (sexual, cultural, or other), because ethnographic approaches to language and identity are focused more on 'thickness' of description than on broad 'samples' of societies or communities. Thus, while I also acknowledge the partiality or perspective which results from my working with a relatively small group of participants in each site (eleven–twelve) and from my focus only on relatively young, male-identified Han individuals from megacity urban contexts. I do not see this as a methodological limitation but as a part of the nature of the study. Also, in terms of class, it is notable that participants were all either in postgraduate education or at an early career stage in relatively well-paid jobs, and that they were all students or graduates of leading universities (a short biography of the participants featured in this Element is given in the appendix). These factors were potentially significant in terms of the sense of socially stratified identity which may have been shared amongst them, and perhaps also in terms of their senses of belonging to a nation, ethnicity or other broadly delimited community, such as the queer/gay/*tongzhi*.

None of these similarities in social background are considered a hindrance to research from an ethnographic point of view. On the contrary, they are considered in context, in light of the extended participant observation which focused more on the nuances of individual cases within a social group. In fact, the variation in life stories and articulations of queer identity that I noted amongst even this small group of somewhat socially homogenous participants is centrally important to my deconstructionist and discursive-sociocultural arguments. For example, I focus on the things participants said that seemed to reflect their individualised and/or situational approaches to the forces of tradition and modernity, and to the significant yet not all-powerful influence of globalised models of 'gay' life (Oswin, 2006).

3.4 Discourse Analysis, Ethnography and Interviews

The data in this Element are taken from seven 60–90-minute semi-structured interviews carried out with some of the men I engaged with towards the end of their involvement in the project. Interview transcripts were first coded thematically and then analysed qualitatively in terms of discourse and positioning, as will be demonstrated in Section 4. I carried out similar interviews with all twenty-three key participants as a means of reflecting and expanding upon themes that had arisen during the six–nine-month period of engagement with each of them. To remain consistent with a semi-structured interview approach, I made significant efforts to allow them to take the lead wherever possible and I left the choice between Mandarin and English with them (see appendix 2 for a discussion of guiding interview themes).

I am strongly aware of issues concerning the sole use of interviewing as a research method. This is especially important when interviewees' personal and social backgrounds are not fully accounted for, and if they are uncritically accepted as cultural/societal/community representatives. Furthermore, people sometimes describe their lives in ways which differ from their actual practice. Also, what they say is not always accurately representative of views and practices in their communities/societies. For these reasons, this was not an interview-based project overall. On the contrary, the specific data types to be collected were not defined in advance, and the general approach to data collection was quite open. As noted above, the interviews were only a part of a much broader period of extended engagement in Chengdu and Taipei, entailing visits to various physical and online spaces, whether queer-specific or not, and engaging face to face in as many ways as possible with participants, friends, acquaintances and others I met along the way. Data collection also included making extensive field notes, gathering printed material and taking photographs of scenes, locations, items and people, both when with participants and when I was alone. This reflects the centrally ethnographic orientation of my work and my wide-ranging, grounded research aim of identifying diverse ideological traces related to the performance of Sinophone queer sexuality.

Accordingly, the interviews were recorded mainly as a means of reflecting on my field notes and other forms of data. The interview data used herein can therefore be seen as a kind of 'easy access' linguistic crystallisation of the broader themes in identity work and ideological navigation that my use of ethnographic methods established. Indeed, although written (and/or transcribed) texts provide perhaps the most easily accessible examples of the kind of ideological traces I was looking for in language use, my analytical choices were based on a less quantifiable, perceived recurrence of certain themes, and sociolinguistic moves, over an extended stay in each location. Broadly then, I followed De Fina (2013: 46) in assuming that:

> Establishing the relevance of Discourses to local identity displays involves paying attention to recurring patterns in data from the same community. At the same time, understanding what these Discourses are (their contents, semantics, values attached etc.), involves having access to ethnographic data and knowledge.

3.5 Data Set and Data Types

Developing the approach described above the project data I gathered consisted of the stories, linguistic styles, stances and vocabulary which seemed salient and discursively significant amongst those with whom I interacted. Specifically the data-collection process included identifying recurring patterns of word use, stories, linguistic styles, vocabulary and stances potentially indexical of corresponding interpretive frameworks. For example, as discussed in detail in Section 4.3, I found the word *hexie* in Mandarin (and *harmony* in English) to be especially common when queer people described themselves as a certain type of person and/or when they characterised the ethnic and/or national community to which they stated belonging. Although quantifying the occurrence of such terms numerically is not part of the methodology I employ, I do assume a degree of 'researcher licence' in positing a discursive salience of associated notions. However, the observations I make on this basis all come with a reflexive caveat: my aim is to trace the navigation of ideological and cultural influence only from my own consciously subjective position. Furthermore, as discussed above, the focus is on the machinations of ideological navigation only in certain specific cases, rather than on trying to draw broad conclusions objectively about lived realities across a given group.

3.6 Project Motivations and Reflexivity

Following ethnographic norms and aware of the fundamentally two-way nature of research interactions, I remained keenly conscious of the relevance of factors such as my white privilege, my English-as-first-language status and my links to relatively powerful British academic institutions. These are very real manifestations of the fundamentally unequal global system and, as such, I remained alert to their potential effects on my interactions with participants, and the project overall. Positioning theory is very much relevant here because it helps demonstrate the two-way nature of interaction and its effects on identity work. Specifically, the words and actions of both myself and those with whom I engaged reflect the positions we took up, and these were implicitly ratified (and, less often, rejected) by the communicative other in each moment of interaction (Gee, 2014 [1999]). In all cases, some of these positions will have been relatively stable across the given periods of interaction. Other positions may have been somewhat more emergent and temporary in nature and shifted according to the specifics of any one social situation and according to which particular person I was engaging with. For example, I was never entirely responsible for my positioning as a friend, which I quite consciously aimed to perform through both my words and my actions, because my interactions with participants always entailed both my own identifying *and* being identified (or perhaps not) in a certain way.

In addition, although I am aware of the potential for my work to be interpreted through the lens of 'white saviour' stereotypes with which white individuals working on non-white communities are sometimes stigmatised, this project was motivated less by culturally arrogant reasons of 'saving' the other than by the often poignant stories of dear friends, research participants and acquaintances I met during my many years in mainland China, many of whom had struggled significantly with related issues. Furthermore, it was also centrally motivated by the fact that related academic work tends to be comparatively difficult for locally based researchers to undertake and publish because of widespread editorial vetting, self-censorship and frequent rejection of related publications on grounds of 'respectability' and 'sensitivity' (Cui, 2023; Ho, 2010; Kong, 2016).

It is perhaps also notable that whilst I lived in mainland China, I put considerable effort into learning Mandarin, understanding local culture and making genuine local connections. In addition, my extensive work as a university teacher during this period entailed engagement with very large numbers of ethnically Chinese students and colleagues not only from all over mainland China but also from Taiwan, Hong Kong, Malaysia and Singapore. I trust that this experience, along with my extended period of residence in the region, mitigated the limitations of my 'cultural outsider' status to some extent. It is also relevant that, at times, the interplay of my outsider 'identity' with other 'identities' and identifications, such as as 'queer' and 'male', meant that the relevant distinction between outside and inside with reference to the communities participants identified as part of was sometimes far from clear. That is, my identification as male and queer might have led to a sense of comfort or social connection for participants who identified in the same way, as might other positions related to, for example, age, socioeconomic background or even social and academic interests. In fact, a combination of such shared identifications may have made me seem like more of an 'insider' to some participants than some hypothetical other who identified as Chinese, but as socially distinct from them on other levels of identity. Furthermore, from an ethnographic point of view, 'outsider' status is not seen as a barrier to effective research anyway. Instead this and other aspects of my own identity work are considered here as part of the 'thick' detail of culture and identity and as a central part of the situated identity work emerging in the cases I analyse.

Another key aspect of my reflexive approach is to recognise that a deconstructionist approach runs the risk of dissolving the categories through which privilege is produced and reproduced. For example, highlighting the social complexity under the term 'Western' could potentially eclipse the continuing global hegemony of powerful governments, companies and institutions from Western/Global North countries, from which my own white and British privileges partly stem. However, while culturalist dichotomies such as East/West and Global North/South, and indeed Chinese/Western, are very much appropriate for analysing such geopolitical injustices, I argue they tend to be somewhat overused when it comes to the analysis of queer identity, especially in Sinophone cultural contexts (see also Freestone, 2023, 2024). This is why I frame my work in terms of identity work and discourse systems as opposed to 'identities' delimited in national or cultural terms, with a view to a fuller acknowledgement of the mutually constitutive nature of global cultural flows (see also Oswin, 2006). Thus, instead of implicitly dismissing Western geopolitical hegemony, I consider it alongside power imbalances of all kinds, including those pertaining to privileges like that of male-identified over female- and trans-identified individuals, urban over rural citizens (Rofel, 2007), the socio-economically and/or educationally privileged over those who are not, and conventionally masculine over effeminate queer males (Russell, 2021).

4 Language and Queer Sinophone Identity Work in Taipei and Chengdu

4.1 Overview

In this section, I draw on the theoretical and methodological perspective described in previous sections as I analyse examples of identity work. In turn, I chart the situated navigation of pertinent discourse systems, with a view to deconstructing common notions of cultural and sexual identity.

4.2 Queer Sinophone Identity Work, Chinese Culture and *Hexie* (Harmony)

As with other cultural, national and ethnic labels, 'Chinese culture' and 'being Chinese' are terms which are often taken to have relatively stable semantic reference but which, from my discursive-sociocultural perspective, are also quite arbitrary and fluid in some ways. As such, their use by people like the men I engaged with often seemed to pertain both to their relatively stable, deep-rooted understandings of self *and* to their more emergent, situated identity work. From this perspective, the use of such terms inevitably entailed the individualised and context-specific navigation of underlying social and structural influences, which is arguably often much less uniform than commonly assumed, amongst a given cultural group. As such, these terms are especially pertinent to the questions of language, ideology and identity that I aim to elucidate in this project overall.

Furthermore, the notions of 'Chinese culture' and 'being Chinese' that participants frequently drew upon seem to be an ideal starting point for a discussion of positioning and identity work. Given the complexities of national, regional and ethnic belonging in mainland China and Taiwan and across the broader Sinophone cultural sphere, these notions serve as especially clear examples of presumed self-evident but actually complex 'identities'. Indeed, I chose Taipei and Chengdu as research sites not only for reasons of comparative ethnographic interest, but also to make a theoretical point about the nature of ideology, the instability of spuriously stable cultural notions and the crucial role of language in identity work. My key point here is that 'Chinese' can mean very different things to different people. Moreover, while there is undoubtedly something relevant and tangible called 'Chinese culture' that significantly affects communication and identity work, associated senses of belonging to associated communities inevitably signify different things to different people. In addition, these become relevant to varying extents and in varied ways, in diverse communicative situations.

The first extract I will discuss is drawn from an interview with Walter, a twenty-six-year-old PhD student, recorded while he and I were discussing approaches to queer visibility in a café in downtown Chengdu.[7] As with all other participants, we had already socialised together regularly for many months and had become good friends. Also, like all of them, Walter was queer male-identified, Han, highly educated, comfortably bilingual and a long-term resident of this relatively cosmopolitan megacity (see appendix 1

---

[7] All participant names are pseudonyms, chosen in Mandarin or English respectively, to reflect the participants' own choice of language in presenting themselves.

for more detailed biographies). Importantly, I see these and other such relatively stable aspects of his and other participants' 'identities' as potentially equally significant to his performance of self as his 'being' (i.e. identifying as) Chinese. That is, although social norms associated with his ethnic/national identity would certainly have been relevant to what he said and did, the relative importance of all the other identities/identifications I mention here (as well as others not mentioned) would depend upon many additional factors. These factors include, but are not limited to, the place he was in, the people present and various aspects of his personality and life story.

In the section of the interview cited in what follows, Walter and I built on related discussions of LGBTQ+ politics and Chinese culture in our previous conversations. At this point in the conversation, he had just said that he thought that Chinese queer-identified people were oriented more towards 'being normal' than pushing for social change (see also Freestone, 2024).

Excerpt 1

1 Phil: Do you think it's a problem, people
            just wanna be normal and don't do
            anything about this?
2 Walter: That's kind of success, at least
            we're not live in pain, every time! ... if
            you are strong enough, you can have a, a
            wider way to solve it, the Chinese way ...
            not so violence but ... smarter ...
            too many activities
            makes things tense, turns into worse ...
            better keep harmony

This excerpt is centrally relevant to the current themes because it can be taken as indexical of Walter's identification, in this moment, with certain discourse systems, or 'ways of seeing the world', which are perceptible through the way he 'speaks about things' (Sunderland, 2004: 28). That is, his linguistic articulation of a sense of cultural and queer self can be understood here in terms of appropriation of complex and diverse structural influences which are fundamentally not as simple as 'ethnically and/or nationally defined cultures'. When it comes to discourse systems, I interpret Walter's use of 'harmony', as well as the overall tone of this moment of conversation, as representing his positioning in alignment with the world view based on balanced relationships between self, others and nature which is central to the philosophy of Confucius. That is, I interpret this as an appropriation of the *Confucian discourse system*

(Scollon et al., 2012). Specifically, I take his use of the word *harmony* in line 10, in the context of the overall excerpt and my broader engagement with him, as entailing the appropriation of the related interpretive framework of assumptions, categories, logics, claims, norms, ethics and values. The pertinent underlying philosophical world view stems from ancient times and has clear cultural residues in the present day, which arguably significantly influence social norms across East Asia (Ambrosio, 2017). Thus, his saying that 'you can have a, a wider way to solve it, not so violence' can be seen in terms of his positioning himself in alignment with a comparatively reticent, harmonious and non-confrontational approach to life corresponds to key concepts in Confucianism, and to interpretive frameworks which still significantly influence social interactions in contemporary times.

Importantly, this is distinct from claiming or implying that because Walter 'is' Chinese, he inevitably always does things in a 'Chinese way'. He may well have taken up different positions in other moments of communication and he may well also have drawn on very different discourse systems, perhaps even within the same conversation. The same is true, of course, for others who tend to identify as Chinese. That is, not everyone who does so takes the same systems of social assumptions for granted in every situation, or indeed at every stage of their lives. In addition, my proposition of discourse appropriation here is not a suggestion that Walter necessarily intended to evoke all the nuanced philosophical connotations of Confucianism simply by using the term 'harmony'. However, my framing this in these terms allows me to chart his response, in this given moment, to some of the structural influences I perceived as salient in his broader social context. In turn, I therefore use it to exemplify the inevitably individualised and situational navigation of locally salient *but not necessarily universally influential* discourse systems, and to set the scene for the rest of the following data analysis. In addition, I use it to demonstrate, in relatively simple terms, how everyday language can reflect individuals' performance of their identities and their drawing on tools from their linguistic/semiotic repertoires.

4.3 Harmony and the Confucian Discourse System

I have chosen to focus on the notion of *hexie* (harmony) because of my perception of its centrality to Confucian philosophy and because of what I perceived to be its widespread salience and influence in everyday life in Sinophone cultural contexts. Firstly, I understand the English term 'harmony' as Walter's translation of the Mandarin term *hexie* not only because it is the most obvious and common translation of the term but also based on my having frequently heard it used in similar ways during my broader experience in the region. It is important to consider, however, that the English gloss can simplify the nuanced localised meanings of the term.

Secondly, I am admittedly assuming a certain degree of researcher authority in suggesting that this discourse system is widespread and prominent, based only on my ethnographic and life experience in the region. However, this is not only my perception. In fact, influential modern philosopher Li Chenyang (2013) states that if only one word were to be chosen to characterise the 'Chinese ideal way' of life, it would be harmony. Somewhat unsurprisingly, then, the prominence of this notion can also be easily traced in educational, institutional and mass media rhetoric.[8] This is exemplified in Hagstrom and Nordin's (2020: 517) citation of a 2009 statement from the PRC State Council, which reads:

> All China's ethnic groups, in the big family of the united motherland and on the basis of equality, are required to ... promote peaceful co-existence and harmonious development, continuously strengthen and develop socialist ethnic relations based on equality, solidarity, mutual assistance and harmony, devote all to the construction of socialist modernization, and make our country strong, our nation thrive and our people happy.

This is not an isolated example, and the general spirit of this statement was very familiar to me as an immigrant in mainland China. As a broad comparison, *hexie* might be understood as having a similar level of discursive salience to that of *democracy* in, for example, the UK. Although no precise equivalence in the social functions of these two terms can be drawn accurately, they are both quite clearly ideologically significant across very broad populations. As such, their patterns of widespread use can be taken to connote the hegemony of corresponding discourse systems and therefore of corresponding interpretive frameworks. In turn, this can be taken as indicative of taken-for-granted world views. These incorporate the kind of 'truths' that I will be referring to as *societal pseudofacts*, such as 'Chinese people are oriented towards social harmony' or 'Western people are oriented towards democracy'. Societal pseudofacts are notions whose connotations tend to be taken as self-evident across a broadly delimited community (be it national, ethnic, sexual or other) and can therefore be taken as indexical of aspects of world view that are hegemonic therein.

---

[8] It is also notable that *hexie* is often employed to reproduce highly normative forms of politics. For example, the term often features in the PRC mainstream and social media in construals of 'abnormal' sexual desire which threatens national and/or cultural 'harmony', whereby queer individuals are seen as enemies of traditional values and sources of social instability (Chang and Ren, 2017; Zheng, 2015).

I should stress that my positing the broader ideological significance of the term 'harmony', and the 'way of seeing the world' it tends to correspond to, in my experience, was not a quantitative exercise. Even if I had tried to quantify the use of the term in some way, such as through corpus linguistics, it would arguably still have been difficult to gauge the actual extent to which such world views are central to the people of mainland China. Furthermore, I would argue that substantiating such a claim would be especially difficult without extended ethnographic engagement with at least some of those people. Thus, as an ethnographer, a sociocultural discourse analyst and a deconstructionist, I did not assume the right to make broad statements about attitudes and social practice amongst a huge population of people based simply on quantitative analysis of the prevalence of one word in certain related contexts. Furthermore, I did not assume that my perceived prominence of this notion corresponded to inevitable alignments with associated (Confucian) world views amongst the boarder population of mainland China. Instead, I focused on how the discourse system of *hexie* was drawn upon (and, of course, sometimes resisted) by individuals in specific conversations like the one I had with Walter. In this sense, the discursive sociocultural approach is fundamentally different to other methodologies.

In addition, while I considered instances of the use of the term *harmony* as potentially indexing a broadly Confucian world view, the aim was not to attribute the appropriation of entire discourse systems to the use of individual words. Instead, my focus is on the situated implications of words like harmony, aiming to exemplify sociolinguistic and ideological processes which are often much more complex than a one-word-to-one-discourse-system correspondence. In fact, there are usually also numerous other linguistic and/or semiotic tools employed alongside such discursive keywords, and these tend to function together, indexing a general orientation towards certain interpretive systems. For example, Walter's use of the notion of the 'Chinese way' and his positioning of self and community as relatively smart, non-confrontational and non-violent can be seen to contribute to an overall sense of orientation towards reticent communication styles (see also Freestone, 2023) and/or non-confrontational approaches to queer politics.

Finally, the notion of Confucianism used here should be acknowledged to be a porous heuristic. For example, although the notion of *hexie* and the vision of society it reflects are central to the writings of Confucius himself, it also features in the writings of various other classic Chinese philosophers (see Halverson et al. 2011). Also, *hexie* was an influential concept long before Confucius. For example, it was a feature of inscriptions on bone and tortoise shells dated as early as the sixteenth century BCE and also of inscriptions on bronze utensils in the Zhou dynasty period (1066–256 BCE) (Li, 2006). Thus, I acknowledge that delimiting the discourse system in question as *Confucian* is a simplification. However, even in deconstructionist analysis, there is a need for some kind of analytical stability. That is, while unpacking the cultural notions we tend to take for granted, it would be unproductive to dissolve all categories of social influence to the point where nothing remains from which to draw analytical conclusions. More broadly, then, the notion of discourse systems is used in this Element to strike the intended balance between productive generalisation and reductive essentialism.

4.4 Positioning, Confucianism and Chinese Culture

A second illustrative case of discursive positioning in identity work came about when notions of Confucianism and Chinese culture were drawn upon together in conversations about participants' sense of self. For example, I had the following conversation during an interview with Tim, a twenty-seven-year-old translator from Taipei (who shared the same broad social identifications which I listed for Walter and others and had known me for a similar amount of time). The conversation was, once again, centred around *being gay* and *Chinese culture*:

Excerpt 2
1   Because we are, like, heavily sedated by
2   Confucianism ... being gay it's like so ...
3   contradictory to ... Chinese culture, like
4   Confucianism ... I dunno ... concept or ideals ... or
5   ideology that you know you are actively fighting
6   against it, but sometimes you lose ... like I
7   cannot come out ... like I still haven't come out
8   to my parents ... that would hurt the harmony
9   in the family ... there's a conservative, it's like,
10 a negative connotation ... they are less acceptive
11 to being different ... which I think has a lot to do
12 with ... oh maybe it's because we are more patriarchal

Firstly, I found this statement by Tim to be indicative of the appropriation of the Confucian discourse system, as in my conversation with Walter. For example, by saying 'being gay it's like so ... contradictory to ... Chinese culture, like Confucianism', Tim can be seen to position himself in distinction from his emic understandings of both Chinese culture and Confucian ideology. He achieves this positioning interactionally, partly by virtue of his implied identification as 'gay' (i.e. when he says 'being gay it's like so contradictory'). He thereby frames being gay as diametrically opposed to all things Chinese and/or Confucian. Also, through the conjunctive use of 'like' here, he seems to equate the notions of Chinese culture and Confucianism, and he uses them together to imply a perceived tendency for traditional viewpoints amongst the relevant community, as he sees it. In doing so, he also positions himself firmly against their 'way of seeing the world', again, as he sees it. In addition, when Tim goes on to say that his parents are 'less acceptive to being different' and that 'sometimes you lose ... I cannot come out', he alludes to the salient issue of normativity (Freestone, 2024; Wei, 2018). Specifically, these words show his sense of constrained agency in the face of strong normative constraints related to sexual orientation. He appears to see these constraints as widespread in the broader community he feels part of, when he suggests that this community (the 'we') is 'heavily sedated'. This is a relatively emotive word choice, implying a strong feeling of subjectification by structural influences, which Tim seems to consider ubiquitous and intrusive within his home community.

In addition, it also seems significant that Tim positions himself as relatively resistant to associated social pressures, by saying that 'you know, you are actively fighting against it'. This sits in contrast to saying that 'I still haven't come out to my parents ... that would hurt the harmony in the family.' and seems to show that he feels significantly constrained by associated moral and ethical expectations, or as he calls them, related 'concept or ideals'. I would delimit these in terms of the Confucian discourse system. Thus, although Tim seems to imply that being 'out' would be desirable for him, he also seems to feel that a reticent approach to sexual identity in the family might be an appropriate linguistic/semiotic tool for avoiding 'hurt' and guarding positive family relationships, which falls in line with broadly Confucian social expectations in line with the discussion of harmony. Considering his words in terms of positioning and discourse systems in this way helps show how he makes active choices in managing such expectations.

More broadly, a discourse and positioning approach also helps in mapping, to some extent, the complexity of associated ideological influences, and highlighting their inevitable diversity. It is not only the Confucian discourse system in play here, since other interpretive frameworks will surely have become significant to Tim, for example, due to his growing up in Taiwan, his socialisation in his own unique family and his relatively cosmopolitan educational and professional and life experience. Thus, Tim's process of ideological navigation in this conversation can also be interpreted in terms of the interplay of the Confucian with other discourse systems. This kind of interplay was, of course, also relevant in Walter's case, but I mention it only now for reasons of clarity, and of logical development of my theoretical position.

One discourse system which can be usefully seen as interacting with the Confucian in a socially signficant way here is what I refer to as the *global queer discourse system* (Freestone, 2024). This corresponds to relatively 'out and proud' approaches to queer identity across the globe, and a globally hegemonic interpretive system which entails related moral and ethical assumptions. When seen in terms of the simultaneous influence of these two key discourse systems, Tim's words can be seen to index his being simultaneously subjectified by and resistant to both. For example, the idea that Tim might want to be 'out' might be seen as common sense, from the perspective of the global queer discourse system. That is, when he says, 'I can't come out,' there is an implied self-evident assumption that he should do so, or that he would want to. The Confucian discourse system, however, might (re)produce the assumption that one needs not 'come out', at least not in the sense of an outright declaration of sexual orientation to all significant others in life.

By extension, the interplay between Confucian and global queer influences here, along with Tim's sociolinguistic response to them, can be seen in terms of his navigation of the diverse structural influences which appear to bring about both social affordances and constraints for him (Jones, 2016). In this sense, the discursive interplay can be taken as a model for the broader tension between structure and agency, and between subjectification and resistance, which is a key theme in post-structuralist and discourse theory (see e.g. De Fina et al., 2006). From this perspective, it is clear how identity work is not always a simple case of taking up one 'identity' (e.g. 'Chinese', 'out'/'not out' or 'straight'/ 'gay') but is more often a case of selecting the communities and viewpoints which we want to foreground, which arise in a given interaction. Furthermore, it is clear that identity work is not simply a process of conforming to or rejecting the presumed self-evident and generalisable norms of one monolithic culture. Of course, it is also important to acknowledge that delimiting Tim's positioning in terms of only two specific discourse systems is a significant simplification of the ideological complexity which pertains to this moment, and to his life more generally. However, even in this simplified form which I present for reasons of clarity, a discursive, sociocultural approach provides important heuristics for avoiding the culturalism which features prominently in the broader body of work on related issues (see discussion section).

4.5 Chinese-ness and Queerness in Taiwan and Mainland China

Another palpable manifestation of the relationship between language, identity and ideology was participants' positioning with reference to certain notions of culture and nationality. For example, despite the cultural commonalities just established, all the men I engaged with in Taiwan consistently positioned themselves as 'Chinese' only in cultural/ethnic (i.e. not national) terms, whereas all those in mainland China positioned themselves consistently as 'Chinese' both ethnically and nationally. I found that these trends emerged across all relevant communicative situations. I feel confident in positing such universality because, due to the political sensitivity of this topic and the stark contrasts in taken-for-granted societal pseudofacts in the respective locations, any examples of Taiwanese participants positioning themselves as Chinese in national terms would have stood out quite prominently. It was especially clear, therefore, that the latter, highly salient identity category tended to carry quite different cultural-national connotations in each respective location. This may seem like a relatively obvious point. It is of course no surprise that when a disputed territory is concerned, people tend to identify in opposing ways, according to their side of the dispute. However, since many prominent works on queer Sinophone issues seem to take Chinese identity and/or Chinese culture as unproblematic and unambiguous (see discussion section and Freestone, 2023, 2024), I do feel the need to emphasise this point now.

Mandarin language identity terms also added a layer of nuance when it came to positioning with reference to notions of culture and nationality. For example, I noted that the term *huaren*, an ethnic label, was frequently used by Taiwanese men as part of the same unanimous tendency to position themselves as Chinese in ethnic but not national terms. More broadly, given the majority political view in Taiwan of the island as a separate national entity to the People's Republic of China (PRC), *huaren* and *taiwanren* (Taiwanese) were the generally preferred terms for national and ethnic identity (cf. Kong, 2019). It is also worth noting that I found similar sociolinguistic identity work to be ubiquitous during my time in Hong Kong, through positioning using the label *hoenggangjan* (Hongkonger). This type of usage can be seen as a politically significant act of identity positioning in both locations, especially in contrast to the term *zhongguoren*, which is ubiquitous in mainland China and which, roughly meaning 'person from China', has clear connotations of nationality as well as ethnicity. Unsurprisingly, it was *zhongguoren* that I found to be most used by the men I met from mainland China when they positioned themselves in terms of ethnic and/or national identity. Interestingly, *huaren* has deep-rooted connotations of Han ethnicity which emerged around the warring states period (475–221 BCE), in connection with the ancient tribes of the Yellow River. *Zhongguoren*, however, is explicitly linked to the mainland Chinese state and emerged after the nationalist revolution.

With reference to the broader sociopolitical questions that are relevant to this study, it is also important that the prominence of the term *huaren* has been explained by Tan (2001) with reference to the process of 'Sinification' in Taiwan (from 1949 to 1987). This process took place under successive presidents from both sides of the political spectrum and began with the rapid dismantling of oppressive military rule in the 1980s. It also entailed the colonialist suppression of aboriginal culture and people (Chun, 1996). This historical process has arguably been a key factor shaping Taiwan's civic-political context, which reflects recent governments' priority of achieving/retaining global recognition as a fundamentally democratic political unit separate from (mainland) China (Kong, 2019). In turn, this has significantly boosted the local drive towards liberalisation and plurality, which pertains to the narratives of democracy and human rights favoured by the DPP, the party which came to power in 2000. Liu (2007: 519) argues that this corresponds to the creation of 'a desperately needed cultural distinction from the People's Republic of China (where human rights continue to be a "sensitive" issue) and its similarities to the United States (which sees itself as the guardian of democratic values)'. This is also reflected in discussions which explicitly relate to issues in the queer community. For example, Kong (2019: 11) suggests that support for the Taiwanese queer community stems, to a significant extent, from an attempt to gain recognition from the international community for Taiwan as a globalised and tolerant society, entailing implicit and conscious distinction from the PRC, which is thereby construed as backward and repressive (see also Ho, 2008). I also found this 'othering' of the PRC, in terms of tolerance and cosmopolitanism related to queer identity, very common in everyday talk in Taiwan (as well as in Hong Kong).

In sum, positioning using national/cultural/ethnic identity terms is a case in point of discursive appropriation/resistance and clearly corresponds to the role of salient interpretive frameworks and societal pseudofacts in shaping speech and social actions, especially when it comes to expressing central senses of belonging. As the current example has shown, this sometimes corresponds to diametrically opposite ways of seeing aspects of the world and to central aspects of individuals' positioning in term of national and ethnic communities.

4.6 Queer Sinophone Identity Work and Notions of 'the West'

Another related sociolinguistic feature of identity work that I found salient, both in research and in daily life, was an interplay between the notions of 'Chinese culture' and 'Western culture'. Whether or not queer topics were being discussed, I found that these notions often arose together in identity work as part of a highly salient system of interpretation based on perceptions of diametrically opposed local and foreign cultures. In fact, whether explicitly mentioned or merely implied, 'the West/Western culture' seemed to be very often taken, in both the research sites, as a convenient benchmark for delimiting what the Sinophone is not. As with the 'othering' of the PRC mentioned in Section 4.5, this speaks to foundational work in Social Identity Theory, which demonstrates how identity is typically based on in-/out-group distinctions, and often as much related to the 'us' and 'them' comparisons which tend to be a fundamental part of identity work around the world. However, what is of central interest here is not the simple fact that humans tend to understand and articulate their sense of belonging in 'them and us' terms, but which particular 'others' tend to become the most salient models of social difference in given communities. On an anecdotal level, I can draw a parallel with comparisons made with the USA amongst the British communities in which I grew up. Of course, it was not the case that everyone always saw the former as a point of cultural comparison, but it did seem that US culture was a highly salient point of reference when it came to articulating a sense of Britishness. As with the case of othering the West in Sinophone communities, this type of positioning often seemed to come hand in hand with divisive cluturalism and sometimes pernicious stereotyping. Resisting this type of paradigm at home and abroad, from my intercultural perspective as a serial immigrant and cultural explorer, is a major motivation for my research, for my personal goal of increasing intercultural understanding and for my quest for true global citizenship.

The following extract demonstrates one example of positioning in East–West terms. It is taken from a conversation with John, a twenty-seven-year-old patent agent from Taipei. As with all the other participants cited, I had known him for a long time at this point and he shared many of the aforementioned relatively stable aspects of identity (i.e. queer male-identified, Han ethnicity, highly educated, comfortably bilingual and a long-term resident of a relatively cosmopolitan megacity).

Excerpt 3

1 I used to be really ... not that open ... but after I read the
2 whole story and I know the Western habit of life like
3 having open relationship or having the free sex ... that
4 kind of stuff ... for us, like ... those who are from Chinese
5 culture ... it's really a different lifestyle ... yeah ... and why
6 not try it ... so after that I have been through open

7	relationship in Taiwan and ... its really new to me and
8	it doesn't bother me at all ... I didn't realise it's also
9	part of Taiwanese culture, maybe more than in China, I
10	guess, because we are more Westernised.

Following the discussion in the previous section, it is notable that John positions himself pronominally within the 'us' of 'Chinese culture' (lines 4–5) and also within the 'us' of 'Taiwanese culture' (line 8). Clearly, however, these are distinct concepts for him, since he also frames the notion of Taiwan in explicit distinction from that of mainland China by saying, 'Taiwanese culture, maybe more than in China' (line 9). However, he still implies a shared 'culture', in terms of approaches to sex, by framing Taiwan and mainland China together, more generally, as a point of contrast to his emic understanding of the Western 'other'. In addition, he directly attributes the difference he perceives between Taiwan and mainland China, in terms of sexual openness, to the influence of the West, saying, 'I guess, because we are more Westernised' (lines 9–10). By positioning himself and his home culture in this way, he can be seen to be drawing on the same interpretive system described previously, whereby 'Western culture' and 'Chinese culture' are understood as fundamentally different, in terms of his perceptions of approaches to what he calls 'free sex' and 'open relationship'. This is therefore another case in point of the fundamental importance of individualised and situational positioning in identity work, especially when taken in the context of the *huaren/zhongguoren* discussion above.

A further related example of positioning in East–West terms came from Bailey, a twenty-eight-year-old finance employee from Taipei, during our discussion in a lounge bar in the city. On this occasion, building on previous discussions based on social and cultural comparison, we discussed the topic of violence against sexual minorities, which I raised with reference to the UK. Bailey responded by saying that:

Excerpt 4

1	The reason why ... it seldom for gay people to be bullied
2	or be beaten is like Chinese culture we never ... admire
3	violence ... even if we hate them, we'll exclude
4	them ... exclude him from our communities, so ... I think the
5	more ... the most awful way for gay people ... if they come
6	out ... they will get excluded from their friends, but they
7	won't get beaten ... it's slightly different to the West.

In discourse terms, I once again understand this framing of Chinese culture in terms of a presumed self-evident orientation towards harmony and non-confrontation in social interaction. That is, when Bailey says, 'Chinese culture we never ... admire violence ... even if we hate them, we'll exclude them', he aligns himself with an interpretive framework of values which is oriented towards both subtlety in communication and non-violent approaches to social others. In this way, he can be seen, like the other men discussed in this Element, to draw upon the Confucian discourse system as part of his articulation of self. More centrally relevant to the current discussion, however, is that the same interpretive system, through which 'the West' and 'Chinese culture' are understood as fundamentally different, appears to be in play here in terms of the way people are seen to treat those they know/perceive to be gay. I will refer to this system as the *discourse system of East–West cultural dichotomies*, which I would also posit as being appropriated in John's case.

In accordance with my broader theoretical and methodological position, my intention here is not to deny nor minimise the importance of broadly generalisable and/or documented social trends related to the level of homophobic violence in each state in question. Indeed, I find some truth in Bailey's cultural comparison, since it seems generally clear to me (anecdotally at least) that the number of instances of homophobic violence would be higher on average in many Western contexts than in Taiwan. This viewpoint is also supported by published work related to a prominence of overt, and sometimes violent, homophobia in, for example, some Southern states of the USA (Davis et al., 2005; National Election Study, 2004), Russia (Tudor, 2018) and certain other locations (e.g. Carrillo, 2007; Graff, 2010; Roseneil and Stoilova, 2016). My key point, however, is that the qualified deconstruction entailed in a discursive-sociocultural approach to identity means also considering such trends in the light of the inevitable diversity of lived realities, both within and across sociopolitically delimited regions.

From this perspective, such social trends can and should indeed be acknowledged. This need not, however, lead us to make overly broad statements about identities or life stories across a wide geographical and/or cultural space. For example, when foundational author Chou Wah-Shan (2000: 106) claims that *tongzhi*, as a broadly generalisable group, 'tend to romanticize the Western world as a lesbigay haven, and are shocked to be informed of the prevalence of gay-bashing and the extent of homophobia in the United States and United Kingdom', I would recognise underlying social trends but also call for qualified deconstruction and recognition of the social diversity in the queer Sinophone community he speaks for. Similarly, instead of taking Bailey's words as representative of distinct social realities in Taiwan and the West respectively, I prefer to understand them in terms of his situated navigation of discourse systems. What seems most analytically significant in my conversation with him, then, is not some substantive regional difference in levels of homophobic violence, but instead the ways in which a presumed self-evident idea of 'the West' is used in positioning.

4.7 Reflexivity, Identity Work and Positioning

As noted in Section 3.6, a key aspect of an ethnographic approach is keen reflexive attention to the role of the researcher. This means that researchers should remain keenly conscious of the cultural, professional and personal 'baggage' they bring to their projects and participants. In addition, from a discursive-sociocultural perspective, it means that researchers should also consider their own and other participants' identities as constructed and sometimes actively negotiated through interaction. For example, my own and others' interpretations of me as white, British-national, male, urban-socialised, queer, pre-1990s-born and immigrant/expatriate (amongst other things) were inevitably relevant to the interactions in question. As such, my own role in identity work in these moments was sometimes also significant, not only because of my inevitably bringing my own identifications/identities to the table, but also because I often brought up issues of cultural comparison in conversation.

A reflexive approach also necessitates attention to the broader sociopolitical factors relevant to my perceived salience of East–West comparisons in identity work. For example, I acknowledge that the deep-rooted influence of colonialism, racism and a fundamentally unfair global system also undoubtedly contributed to the salience of such comparisons. That is, the continuing hegemonic influence of Western powers on the global stage, and the residues of unfair treatment based on race, inevitably push the presence of notions of the West into the lives of people outside of the West. However, while I fully appreciate the gravity of such issues, the focus here is on how individuals draw upon notions as part of their identity work.

Secondly, in mainland China in particular, the prominence of notions of 'the West' which I noted may have been partly due to certain influential state narratives which have remained hegemonic throughout modern local history. These feature a presumed self-evident notion of 'the West' that has been consistently taken as a point of social comparison and often also as an implied reference point for the socially undesirable (Freestone, 2024). Of course, I acknowledge that the same is true of some hegemonic state and media narratives in places like the UK and the USA through which, for example, all things communist and/or Chinese have tended to be construed in similarly negative terms. What is most pertinent to the current discussion, however, is that I found positioning with reference to notions of the West very common across all the Sinophone cultural contexts in which I spent time. This may well have been influenced by these powerful state-level narratives but may also have arisen for other reason, depending on the case in question.

The key point in this section is that I see all project data from a consciously reflexive point of view, with a careful awareness of the mutually constituted nature of identity work. However, based on my broader experience in the region, I would also argue that the type of East–West framing of culture and social practice discussed in the previous section would be quite common even when a Western-identified interlocutor was not present in each moment of communication. Indeed, I believe that it was much more than my own Westernness, or my specific conversational choices, that made this notion so salient among the men I engaged with.

4.8 Queer Sinophone Identity Work and East–West Framings of Family

Another salient theme when considering the articulation of queer Sinophone identity seemed to be associated perceptions of cultural realities related to family. This theme is centrally relevant to the current discussion because, when issues of family arose in relation to queer identity, appropriation of both the Confucian discourse system and that of East–West cultural dichotomies seemed common. This was the case in both research sites and, as with the discourse of harmony and framings of violent homophobia, I found the discussion of family to be especially indicative of widely presumed societal pseudofacts. Thus, this again called for qualified deconstruction of attendant notions of culture, identity and, specifically, of family.

Firstly, I noticed that East–West cultural dichotomies tended to come into play simultaneously with a taken-for-granted cultural centrality of family in Chinese societies, which typically came along with an implication that family is less important in the West. I found this to be a societal pseudofact that was very widely taken for granted amongst participants and many others I interacted with. The presumed centrality of family, in the Chinese case, is also reflected in literature on queer lives, such as in Whyte's (1997: 2) claim of an 'overwhelming Chinese emphasis on obligations to the family'. It came as no surprise to me, in light of the general salience of related cultural schema, that conversations around the theme of family life in Sinophone cultural contexts often also featured such taken-for-granted points of view. I also found it common for them to be associated with presumptions of inevitably rigid and codified family expectations, including that of a son to his parents. What was perhaps more remarkable to me, however, was the frequency of attendant implications about the situation in Western families being self-evidently different. Related themes were part of the conversation cited next, which I had with Peter, a twenty-nine-year-old travel agent from Chengdu.

Excerpt 5
1   It's different for us, in China ... you guys,
2   y'know ... in the West, you can do what you
3   want ... more, like, your parents let you be
4   free to choose ... I mean, like, there's
5   pressure, obviously ... but, um, it's not the
6   same ... like ... if you don't wanna marry it's
7   easier, if you wanna be gay, it's easier ... the
8   family, for us ... it's everything ... like, if we
9   don't do what the family wants, we are
10 screwed ... like, our lifeline is gone ... we will
11 be kicked out ... or they will not want to help us
12 anymore, if we don't do what, like
13 apparently, everyone knows we should do.

Although Peter was making points that resonated with many other conversations I had in mainland China, I was reluctant to take such broad ideas of cultural reality for granted and, instead, aimed again for qualified deconstruction. Indeed, I considered it significant that I had also found many cases in which family seemed to be less important to certain Chinese-identified individuals than might be expected (see also Freestone, 2023). Furthermore, I found many instances where participants who identified as Chinese (ethnically and/or nationally) had distanced themselves from the natal family to varying extents. For example, migration to the big city from rural areas was often a key life choice, as was choosing to live long term in a foreign country and in a number of cases, this was directly linked to avoidance of family. On the other hand, it also seemed relevant that my experience of growing up in the UK presented many examples of life stories where family seemed extremely important to queer individuals, contrary to the parallel societal psuedofacts which lead to hegemonic perceptions of Westerners as inherently less oriented to family as a priority in life. In addition, the East-West dichotomy being drawn upon here did not accord with my knowledge of family culture in some countries in the West which are renowned for the centrality of family, in similar ways to the Chinese example.

Thus I interpret this statement not as a reflection of broadly generalisable social reality in mainland China and/or across Sinophone cultural contexts but instead of Peter's positioning by drawing upon the discourse system of East-West dichotomies, and his concurrent navigation of the *discourse system of filial piety*, which I see as a subsystem of the Confucian discourse system. Specifically, this means I see him drawing upon interpretive frameworks which are widely influential in guiding and reproducing expectations about parent and child in mainland China, Taiwan and across the broader East Asian cultural sphere (Hu and Wang, 2013; Wang et al., 2009). These frameworks pertain to social practices associated with 'being a good son' in the Confucian terms of *xiaoshun* (filial piety) and, in many conversations I had, this corresponded to presumptions of fundamental and self-evident cultural difference from the West. As with the notion of harmony discussed earlier, a sociocultural discourse analyst would view related identity work in terms of how associated societal pseudofacts and interpretive frameworks are appropriated or resisted when the topic of family is being discussed. Thus Peter's positioning in this excerpt is understood here not in terms of monolithic cultural or structural forces which uniformly influence social actions across a broad community, but instead in terms of discourse systems that individuals draw upon to achieve certain identity effects in certain situated conversations.

4.9 *Tongzhi* versus Western Queer Politics: A Qualified Deconstruction

As noted in my introduction, the choice to work on this project's central themes is partly driven by a desire to contribute to queer emancipation in local communities. For the avoidance of any ambiguity, I define queer emancipation as the process of helping more sexually/gender different people to live and love without political, cultural and/or social constraints on their sexual and romantic lives. Perhaps unsurprisingly, this was a salient topic in project data and I therefore find it important to link the discussion in the previous sections with broader questions of how associated social change can be fostered in Taiwan, mainland China and perhaps elsewhere. For example, Walter's conversational moves in the cited excerpt struck me as relevant to key questions of LGBTQ+ politics and provided relatively accessible examples of positioning with reference to salient interpretive frameworks. When he said, 'if you are strong enough, you can have a, a wider way to solve it, the Chinese way ... not so violence but ... smarter ... too many activities makes things tense, turns into worse ... ', he seemed to echo a societal pseudofact according to which LGBTQ+ activism and advocacy in Sinophone contexts is best oriented towards societal harmony, as opposed to confrontation. For me, this demonstrated a powerful interpretive framework which takes as self-evident a 'Chinese' orientation to harmony and confrontation avoidance both on the personal level already discussed and on a the broader level of politics and advocacy.

Thus, Walter's employment of the notion of the 'Chinese way' can also be seen as his positioning himself in alignment with the discourse of East–West cultural dichotomies and with an approach to queer emancipation which he seems to indirectly compare to that of the West. Specifically, by describing the approach he associated with his own community as 'not so violence but . . . smarter' because 'too many activities makes things tense', he seems to be advocating a broadly reticent and non-confrontational approach to LGBTQ+ identity politics, in implied distinction from mine, as interlocutor. More broadly, I interpreted Walter's positioning in these terms as pertinent to assumptions that the broad population labelled as 'Chinese gays' or *tongzhi* will always accord to a conveniently generalisable approach to achieving queer emancipation: one which is non-confrontational and therefore significantly different to that of the West. It is perhaps worth reiterating my broader position here. I am not, of course, claiming that there is no difference between the broader queer emancipation movements in what can be loosely perceived as the 'Chinese' and 'Western' cases. Instead, I am drawing attention to the inevitable diversity of associated political orientations, social actions and identity work within and across the huge variety of relevant countries, cultural contexts and individual cases on both sides of the presumed East-West divide. Moreover, I am drawing attention to Walter's framing of approaches to LGBTQ+ politics in terms of a presumed self-evident 'Chinese way', which seems to eclipse some of this diversity, and which also demonstrates his positioning in implied 'them and us' terms. I interpreted this, on the basis of the many similar conversations I had had during my research and life experience, as an implied East vs. West reference.

Another related example can be seen in the following conversation which I had with Dave, a twenty-four-year-old teacher from Chengdu, in a teahouse we often visited. Again, Dave shared the key aspects of sociocultural background mentioned in Walter and others' cases. When discussing the extent to which he felt a need to be 'out' to friends and family, he said:

Excerpt 6
1   It's like . . . I'm not proud but I think now I'm
2   living good . . . I think a better way is that,
3   live better, to make everyone say, 'wow he's a
4   good person' . . . that's more important . . .

I understood the statement 'I'm not proud' as a reference to the narratives of 'pride' that characterise the relatively outgoing and individualistic models of queer identity typically associated with the 'gay rights' movement consolidated by events like the Stonewall riots in the USA. Importantly, however, in the contemporary world, this model corresponds to forms of queer identity work which are prominent in countless LGBTQ+ lives not only in broadly Western contexts, but also in contexts around the world.

In terms of the positioning in Dave's statement, however, what we see is him describing himself in opposition to those he sees as 'proud' and thereby positioning himself in distinction from a discourse system (and interpretive framework) which assumes that overtly indexing one's queer sexual orientation is broadly desirable. Specifically, I understood his statement that 'I'm not proud . . . ' not as an index of his presumed 'non-Western-ness', but instead as a moment of alignment with what I will be referring to as the *post-gay* discourse system, which is itself globalised. This system corresponds to a broadly homonormative interpretive framework which entails rejecting, at least to some extent, models of queer identity performance and LGBTQ+ politics which are overtly visible, and which may be considered by some as confrontational. This system produces and reproduces oppositional stances to perceived hegemonic norms of a 'proud' contemporary queer society (Russell et al., 2009). Jones (2018) also noted this type of viewpoint being expressed by attendees of a UK youth group, as reflected in a quote – 'I'm not proud, I'm just gay' – from one participant in her study, which is also the article's title.[9] The relevant point here is that, just as the participants in Jones' study should not necessarily be taken as broadly representative of British youth culture, Dave should not be taken as 'being' the way he is simply because he 'is Chinese'. Indeed, by extension, no other such moment of appropriation of the post-gay discourse system should be mistaken for a cultural inevitability. Instead, although globally hegemonic, the 'proud' stance against which individuals might position themselves (and/or the 'post-gay' discourse system that they might align themselves with) can arise in any global location and, as such, is arguably best investigated in the context of the specific sociopolitical contexts, life stories and communicative moments in which they are drawn upon.

It is also interesting that this kind of 'not proud' positioning seems to echo the positioning in terms of 'harmony' which we saw in excerpts 1 and 2. That is, all these moments of positioning seem to entail an articulation of the self as someone who prefers not to 'shout' about their queerness (i.e. be actively visible as queer-identified). The ideological influences that seem to be most relevant here, however, are not easily attributed to a single source, be that geographical or cultural. So, it came as no surprise that I encountered very many examples of 'out' and 'proud' positioning amongst young, relatively cosmopolitan individuals in Sinophone contexts (see Freestone 2023 for further examples). For me, this once again highlighted the inevitable diversity of corresponding identity work, despite the hegemony of certain discourse systems like the post-gay and the Confucian.

---

[9] See also Savin-Williams (2005).

Thus, although the global historical significance of events leading to and including the Stonewall riots in the USA and the subsequently galvanised gay rights movement should not be overlooked, the mutually constitutive nature of discursive influences from diverse global regions should also be emphasised in any analysis of queer identity in non-Western contexts. In addition, it should be recognised that decisions on whether to be 'out' or 'not out' and/or 'proud' or 'not proud' should be understood as made in response to specific social situations and as inevitably shifting across moments and lifetimes. This also draws attention to the fact that many instances of 'proud' (i.e. actively visible) steps towards queer emancipation will inevitably have emerged outside 'the West', whether on an individual or a group level and, conversely, that many comparatively 'reticent' steps have been taken in locations within it. In this light, the interplay between Dave's performed sense of Chinese-ness and his alignment with/distancing from post-gay narratives of LGBTQ+ politics can be taken as exemplary of the typical ideological complexity of contemporary queer lives, and especially the lives of modern, cosmopolitan, megacity-urban queers in Sinophone cultural contexts. Furthermore, the whole notion of 'being out' (or being visible as queer) is itself highly situational and unstable. That is, one may well be 'out' and/or 'proud' by acknowledging queer sexuality to certain specific others and in certain specific situations but, not in others (Freestone, 2023).

A final relevant example came from Dan, a twenty-four-year-old accountant from Chengdu who, once again, knew me well at the time and shared the aforementioned aspects of relatively stable identity/identification as the other participants. He said that:

Excerpt 7
1 Dan: Y'know, Chinese people, y'know, don't have
the sense of fight, actually, mm, yeah,
it's a culture thing
2 Phil: Why don't they have a sense of fight?
3 Dan: I dunno, it's a cultural thing, people
just don't like chaos
4 Phil: Do you think its cultural or is it political?
5 Dan: Well, because, y'know, the cultural things
Will affect the political things, so both
things yes.

Firstly, like the other participants, Dan seems to see queer politics in cultural terms, understanding 'the Chinese people' as having a unique and predictable approach. One novel aspect of Dan's positioning, however, is his construal of 'the

Chinese' as having no 'sense of fight'. This again seems to echo the aforementioned construals of Chinese culture in terms such as non-confrontational and harmonious, which also seemed to imply a characteristic opposition to *fighting*. Similarly, Wei (2021: 328–329) claims that 'many ordinary *tongzhi* are politically docile and indifferent, uninterested in rights advocacy or confrontational queer politics'. This speaks to emergent social trends of youth non-participation, both in politics and also in other aspects of life such as parenthood, which are framed as 'lying flat' (*tangping*). However, both Wei's and Dan's statements are ripe for qualified deconstruction. The notions of 'many ordinary *tongzhi*' and 'Chinese people', in a society as vast and culturally diverse as mainland China, need to be problematised. For example, there are also many cases where those who tend to identify as *tongzhi* do, in fact, take actions to change society in ways that entail visible and active resistance to political, legal and social constraints on queer people (see Bao 2018 for examples).

Furthermore, the framing of a localised and presumed self-evident 'Chinese' approach to social struggle as inherently harmonious and non-confrontational, both by Wei (2021) and Dan, is problematic not only in terms of the inevitable diversity of individual approaches that it eclipses, but also when some of the numerous militant and violent political moments in broader Chinese history are considered. For example, many instances of highly confrontational sociopolitical resistance, often based around the rights of a certain group united under a certain identity term, have emerged in mainland China in relatively recent history, such as the June 4 Movement and the communist revolution of 1949. Also, the corresponding implication that no aspects of the queer emancipation movement across the modern history of 'the West' (which is, like China, a vast and diverse cultural and geographical space) have been non-confrontational and harmonious is, at best, blinkered.

It is also of sociolinguistic interest to note, that this excerpt features some interesting individual words which can be taken, in this context of use, as indicative of relevant discourse systems. The first is luan (chaos) which I often found to emerge in interplay with the opposing notion of wending (stability). The salience and social significance of these notions corresponds to Zheng's (2015: 57) discussion of the stigmatising framing of queer people, in public and media narratives in mainland China, as sources of social chaos and disorder. The political implications and historical persistence of such narratives are also reflected in Anagnost and Comaroff's (1997: 275) discussion of 'narrative(s) of despair' which they found to be key strategies used in mainland China to address 'concerns about stability and social control' by 'invok(ing) the fear of chaos' and thereby producing 'willed consent' for an authoritarian state. However, the implications of these notions are not universal and can reflect quite divergent attitudes and social perceptions. This is why it is useful to consider their use only as reflecting the navigation, in situated moments of communication, of powerful structural influences salient in given social contexts. In Dan's speech cited here, then, I see these notions as functioning in a similar way to the notion of hexie – that is, as appropriations of the Confucian discourse system. This is because they pertain directly to the aforementioned ideas of balance between society and nature that are central to Confucian philosophy, which Dave can be seen to align himself here through the stance he takes up on 'Chinese people'.

5 Discussion

As should be clear from the preceding sections, this Element is a conscious response to approaches to sexuality, identity and culture which are based on presumed monolithic cultural influences and/or overgeneralised claims and implications about social practice across broadly delimited communities. Of course, it should also be clear that I acknowledge that the societies of Taiwan and mainland China (and, by extension, other Sinophone contexts) do have some pertinent shared cultural, social and philosophical background. Indeed the influence of this shared background has been acknowledged herein as having tangible implications for everyday conversation, and therefore for everyday identity work. Thus, rather than rejecting it entirely, I build upon work which posits or assumes a tangible Chinese way of doing and being queer. Related perspectives feature in many key foundational works on related topics in the mainland China case, such as Chou (2000), Hinsch (1990), Ho (2010) Li (1998; with Wang, 1992) and Zhang (1994, 2005; Zhang et al., 2008), and they also remain highly influential in more recent work, as I discuss elsewhere (Freestone, 2023, 2024). Meanwhile, I am especially indebted to work which, in contrast, questions the universality of 'Chineseness' and perceptively charts the sociopolitical and sociocultural complexities of the broader queer Sinophone context (e.g. Chiang and Heinrich, 2013; Chiang and Wong, 2020; Chun, 2017; Liu, 2015). Some other related work engages, mostly in passing, with post-structuralist and/or deconstructionist approaches to identity but remains based on presumed monolithic cultural and/ or sociopolitical influences, and in turn reproduces associated culturalist dichotomies. Clear cases in point are Kong (2023) and Bao (2018), the latter of which I discuss in what follows with a view to consolidating the key points made in the preceding sections. Of course, this comes with an acknowledgement of the great value of Bao's extensive work and its leading role in developing the field of research on queer mainland China (see e.g. Bao, 2018, 2020).

Firstly Bao (2018) unpacks *tongzhi* as 'queer comrades' in an insightful play on the varied connotations of the Chinese characters. However, despite claiming alignment with related postmodernist work, and despite initially describing this label as a floating signifier, he arguably goes on to overlook some of the key value of such work by giving a rather exceptionalist depiction of the mainland Chinese queer emancipation movement, framed under this identity label. For me, this follows the same pattern of drawing on societal pseudofacts and cultural dichotomies discussed in the previous sections. Bao (2018: 3) suggests that this movement is unique in its purportedly Chinese socialist approach to queer politics, since 'the Socialist past laid the foundation and provided the inspiration for contemporary Chinese gay identity and queer politics'. He thereby construes this approach as fundamentally different to that in other places (and especially the West), claiming 'a non-liberal alternative to the Euro American model of queer emancipation grounded in liberal values of privacy, tolerance, individual rights, and diversity' (Bao, 2018: 3). However, this discussion seems to come without a clear demonstration of what makes the instances of queer resistance he describes 'non-liberal' or *not* based on a desire for privacy, individual rights and diversity. Such instances include a relatively small-scale and individualised campaign against conversion therapy, a stand-off between queer-identified males and police in a public park (based around calls for community rights) and an LGBTQ+ film movement, all of which seem to have much in common with other emancipation movements around the world, and across history. This seems similarly clear when it comes to the underlying spirit of grassroots resistance, which I would argue does not, in fact, depend on a socialist political orientation, whether or not that be one which claims 'Chinese characteristics'.

The relevance of this discussion of Chinese specificity to the cases of participants in the current study and other related authors cited herein should be clear. Indeed, for me, Bao (2018) draws on discourse systems reproducing hegemonic and widely circulating societal pseudofacts about Chinese specificity which, in cases like these, are generalisations that are arguably more problematic than productive. Again, although these may pertain to tangible social, political and cultural contrasts to some extent, they are perhaps best also understood in light of the inherent diversity which also inevitably exists, in terms of approaches to identity and queer politics within any society, and especially amongst a population as vast as that of mainland China.

In addition, when Bao (2018: 7) sets up *tongzhi* as 'a mode of becoming rather than a mode of being', he claims that the term is, in itself, performative and implies that it therefore automatically brings a certain type of identity and politics into being when it is used. However, from a discursive-sociocultural point of view, *all* identity categories are, in fact, temporary subject positions taken up (performed) in situated communications. Therefore, an individual's ideological alignment with a political stance or movement through their identification with a given term is certainly not inevitable but, instead, emerges in only some individual life stories and, indeed, in only some communicative situations. In line with this, I found highly varied social and political orientations and a corresponding diversity of usages of identity labels and identity positions, even across the small section of the queer community that I engaged with in mainland China. This included *tongzhi* being a term used (or rejected) in distinct ways, by different people, in different situations (see also Zhou, 2022). This is also exemplified by the active resistance to the term *tongzhi* within activist communities in Hong Kong where, according to Wong (2005), individuals and community groups consciously distanced themselves from the communist connotations of the word, and thereby from mainland China and its social and political system, after having originally reclaimed the term within their very community in the 1980s/1990s.

Thus, while we should certainly recognise the influential trends in advocacy and campaigning movements that the term sometimes connotes, it should also be actively recognised that some (or even many) of those who identify as *tongzhi* may well not speak and act in alignment with them especially in their mainland Chinese form. Indeed, some of them might position themselves firmly against such approaches. However, this fluidity of *tonzghi*, as a label used in diverse ways in identity work, is arguably lost in Bao (2018), due to his pursuit of a somewhat romanticised and essentialist specificity of the mainland Chinese case, which he frames under this label, presuming its universal connotations for all who identify with it, in queer terms. Thus, his important description of relevant social trends and localised cultural specificities slips into problematic overgeneralisation and divisive culturalism, with *tongzhi* being taken as representative of a vast and diverse social group's supposedly universal social, political and/or philosophical orientation, in every conversation in which the term is used as a queer label.

In these ways, this example serves to consolidate the key arguments I have been making throughout this Element. As we have seen, the associated complexities of queer Sinophone identity tend, in fact, to emerge very clearly on an everyday level when diverse cases are examined over an extended period of time. In addition, we have seen that there are varied discourse systems and corresponding interpretive frameworks which tend to be drawn upon and resisted variously in everyday identity work. This variation raises questions about how accurately such generalised widely models of distinct cultures can be applied in analysis of queer lives (whether activist cultures or ethnic or national cultures). In response, the discursive-sociocultural approach taken up herein insists upon a fuller acknowledgement, firstly, of the diversity of life stories which exists in related communities, secondly, of the mutually constitutive nature of linguistic-cultural-ideological interplay and, thirdly, of the inherently fluid nature of identity. This seems especially important in relatively cosmopolitan lives like those of the participants discussed herein.

6 Conclusion

In this Element, I have analysed the sociolinguistic navigation of structural influence in the everyday identity work of seven queer male-identified individuals in Chengdu and Taipei using a discursive-sociocultural approach. I have considered structural influences on individuals in terms of the emergent communicative process through which they perform their somewhat stable, yet ultimately fluid 'selves'. Thus, my analysis of issues related to sexuality, identity and culture has not only been a question of broad cultural and/or sociopolitical norms (whether implied or explicit). Instead, I have shown how not all the individuals and communities typically referred to by broad everyday identity labels navigate ideological influences in the same ways. I have also shown that an analytical reliance on such ostensibly stable terms can lead to an oversight of diversity and/or to oversimplification of the multifaceted nature of each individual's identity work. Furthermore, I have argued that accounting for these social complexities is especially important in the case of the highly mediated and globalised social worlds of relatively young, urban and educated megacity-urban residents in contemporary times.

This Element is therefore a call for a better balance between productive generalisation and reductive essentialism, whereby more diversity within and across communities in different geographical locations is acknowledged without losing sight of important and tangible social trends. In this way, it has not only contributed to the field of queer linguistics by raising these themes in the context of Sinophone sexual minority communities but has also offered a relatively novel methodological and theoretical perspective to the existing body of work on queer lives in mainland China, Taiwan and the broader Sinophone sphere. Its discussion of issues of LGBTQ+ politics and queer emancipation not only exemplifies the process of sociolinguistic positioning in identity work, but also highlights how this process is inflected by complex discursive influences which individuals navigate, consciously and unconsciously, on an everyday level. This has implications for sociolinguistics, sociology and anthropology because reflecting on such issues through the discursive-sociocultural lens arguably facilitates more accurate charting of the actual situated effects of ideological forces relevant to scholars of queer cultures in all such disciplines. Furthermore, when we discuss positioning in specific conversations, as opposed to positing the presumed predictable social effects of broad social and cultural forces, the multi-sited, highly classed and highly individualised nature of struggles for queer emancipation is foregrounded. As such, more of the diversity under umbrella identity terms like 'gay', 'Chinese' and 'Western' can be accounted for, along with the fluid parameters of sociopolitical and socio-economic influence on individual life stories.

Appendices
Appendix 1: Participant Biographies

As noted in the main body of the Element, all participants cited herein were queer male-identified, Han, educated to at least undergraduate level, comfortably bilingual and long-term residents of Chengdu and Taipei. They were not selected as representative of any given community but instead because their words, in certain moments, illuminated the themes central to the project. The following aspects of their life stories may also be considered relevant:

(1) 'Walter', a twenty-six-year-old PhD student originally from north-east China, moved to Chengdu at eighteen years old, with his family, and still lived with them at the time of the project. He identified as gay and said he always used the English term for self-identification.

(2) 'Tim', a twenty-seven-year-old translator from Taipei, had lived in the city all his life. He had lived separately from his family since twenty-three years of age. He identified as gay and said he used various terms for self-identification, both Mandarin and English.

(3) 'John', a twenty-seven-year-old patent agent from Taipei, was originally from Hualien in eastern Taiwan. He moved to Taipei at twenty-one and had lived separately from his family since then. He identified as gay and said he always used the English term for self-identification.

(4) 'Bailey', a twenty-eight-year-old finance employee from Taipei, had lived in the city all his life. He had lived separately from his family since twenty-five years of age. He identified as gay and said he always used the English term for self-identification.

(5) 'Peter', a twenty-nine-year-old travel agent from Chengdu, had lived in the city all his life and separately from his family since twenty-six years of age. He identified as gay and said he used various terms for self-identification, both Mandarin and English.

(6) 'Dave', a twenty-four-year-old teacher from Chengdu, had lived in the city all his life and still lived with his parents there at the time of the project. He identified as gay and said he used various terms for self-identification, both Mandarin and English.

(7) 'Dan', a twenty-four-year-old accountant from Chengdu, was originally from Beijing; he had moved to Chengdu at eighteen for university and stayed

there since then. He lived separately from his family. He identified as gay and said he always used the English term for self-identification.[1]

Appendix 2: Example Semi-Structured Interview Questions

For reasons of contextualisation and with a view to potential replication of parts of this study, the following are provided as examples of the questions and themes which came to be salient in project interviews. As noted, these interviews came after a long period of engagement with participants, and were used to consolidate and clarify the viewpoints and themes participants themselves had foregrounded during our broader interactions. As the approach to interviews was semi-structured, however, there was no pre-formulated question list. The thematic focus shifted continually both during the project overall and within individual interviews and other discussions. Furthermore, significant and concerted effort was made to allow participants to take the lead in all project phases, and for them to shape not only the project interactions, but also our general socialisation patterns.

1. Background

    How old are you?
    What is your job?
    Where do you live now and how long have you lived there?
    Have you spent any time in other regions/countries? If so, why?
    Shall I use your real name or a fake name in my writing?
    May I share your data?

2. Socialisation

    Is the city you live in a good place for queer people? Why/why not?
    How do you meet other queer men?
    Do you hang out with the queer people you know? If so, what do you do?
    What kind of 'gay' places do you go to? Why/why not? How often?
    In your region, are dating applications a more common way of meeting than face to face?
    Do you use such apps? Which ones? Why? How often? What do you use them for?
    Which languages do you use (a) on your profile and (b) in chats?
    Do you post photos? Why/why not? What kind of photos?

---

[1] As noted in section 4.2, all participant names are pseudonyms and reflect the choice of participants to introduce themselves to me using their Englsih names.

3. Community and Geography

    How much do you feel part of the queer community (a connection with a wider group)? Why/why not?
    Are you a 'typical' gay/queer guy? Why/why not?
    Is 'Western gay culture' different to local queer culture?
    Are you 'Westernised'? Are you 'gay in a Western way'?
    How much have the lives of queer people in your region been influenced by 'gay culture' from the West (e.g. politics, fashion, lifestyle)? How about you?

4. Marriage/Coming Out

    How easy is it for queer people to come to terms with their sexuality in your region compared to other parts of the world? Why?
    What are/have been the main sources of pressure in your life? Are any of them related to your sexual identity?
    Have you come out? If so, how? To whom? What were their reactions? If not, why not?
    How would your parents react if you told them you were going to live with a man you loved?
    How much pressure are you under to get married and produce a child? How do/would/will you deal with any such pressure?
    Is it better for same-sex-attracted people to tell their parents about their sexual identity earlier or later?
    What factors affect the decision to 'come out' (or not) in your society?
    How do you feel about adoption by same-gender people? How important is it to you? Will you do it? If so, how? Will it be easy?

5. Attitudes and Social Change

    What do various types of people in different parts of your society think about queer people?
    How do you feel about attitudes to same-sex sexualities in (a) your society in general and (b) your city/region/area in particular?
    To what extent do you want to be 'just like everyone else', or are you proud of being different to mainstream society?
    How can progress towards better lives for queer people in your region be made?
    To what extent should 'coming out' be encouraged in order to increase acceptance of queer sexualities in your region? Why?
    Are LGBTQ+ societies a good thing? How many of them exist in your region? Why?

Are 'Pride' parades a good thing? Are they suitable in your culture and/or region? Why?

Is putting pressure on the government to legalise same-sex marriage a good thing? What about legislation for equal rights (e.g. in the workplace)?

6. Masculinity

What is considered a 'real man' in your country/region? How should they look, behave?

Is 'sissyphobia' a problem in your region?

Do people discriminate against male femininity more than homosexuality in your region?

In terms of sex roles, do you think more ethnically Chinese than Western men are 'bottom'?

Do you think there are lots of 'bottoms' in your society/region? Why/why not?

References

Agerholm, H. (2017, 1 February). Taiwan on verge of becoming first Asian country to allow same sex marriage. *The Independent*. http://bit.ly/4fcCN9a.

Ambrogio, S. (2017). Moral education and ideology: The revival of Confucian values and the harmonious shaping of the new Chinese man. *Asian Studies* 5, 113–135.

Anagnost, A., and Comaroff, J. L. (1997). *National Past-Times: Narrative, Representation, and Power in Modern China*. Durham, NC: Duke University Press.

Bakhtin, M. M. (1986 [1979]). *Speech Genres and Other Late Essays*. Austin: University of Texas Press.

Bao, H. (2020) *Queer China: Lesbian and Gay Literature and Visual Culture under Postsocialism*. London: Routledge.

Bao, H. (2018). *Queer Comrades: Gay Identity and* Tongzhi *Activism in Postsocialist China*. Copenhagen: Nordic Institute of Advanced Studies Press.

Berry, C., Martin, F. and Yue, A. (eds.). (2003). *Mobile Cultures: New Media in Queer Asia*. Durham, NC: Duke University Press.

Bi, L., and D'Agostino, F. (2004). The doctrine of filial piety: A philosophical analysis of the concealment case. *Journal of Chinese Philosophy* 31(4), 451–467.

Block, D. (2022). *Innovations and Challenges in Identity Research*. London: Routledge.

Blommaert, J. (2005). *Discourse: A Critical Introduction*. Cambridge: Cambridge University Press.

Boellstorff, T. D. (2011). But do not identify as gay: A proleptic genealogy of the MSM category. *Cultural Anthropology* 26(2), 287–312.

Bucholtz, M., and Hall, K. (2005). Identity and interaction: A sociocultural linguistic approach. *Discourse Studies* 7(4–5), 585–614.

Bucholtz, M., and Hall, K. (2004). Theorizing identity in language and sexuality research. *Language in Society* 33, 469–515.

Butler, J. (1990). *Gender Trouble: Feminism and the Subversion of Identity*. London: Routledge.

Cao, J., and Lu, X. (2014). A preliminary exploration of the gay movement in mainland China: Legacy, transition, opportunity, and the new media. *Signs: Journal of Women in Culture and Society* 39(4), 840–848.

Carrillo, H. (2007). Imagining modernity: Sexuality, policy and social change in Mexico. *Sexuality Research and Social Policy* 4(3), 74–91.

Cashman, H. R. (2019). What Phoenix's *jotería* is saying: Identity, normativity, resistance. *Language in Society* 48(4), 519–539. https://doi.org/10.1017/S0047404519000411.

Chang, J., and Ren, H. (2017). Keep silent, keep sinful: Mainstream newspapers' representation of gay men and lesbians in contemporary China. *Indian Journal of Gender Studies* 24(3), 317–340.

Chen, K.-H. (2010) *Asia as Method: Toward Deimperialization*. Durham, NC: Duke University Press.

Chen, X., and Ang, P. (2011). The internet police in China: Regulation, scope and myths. In D. Herold and P. Marolt (eds.), *Online Society in China: Creating, Celebrating and Instrumentalising the Online Carnival* (pp. 40–52). London: Routledge.

Cheng, Y. A., Wu, F. C. F. and Adamczyk, A. (2016). Changing attitudes toward homosexuality in Taiwan, 1995–2012. *Chinese Sociological Review* 48(4), 317–345.

Chiang, H., and Heinrich, A. L. (eds.). (2013). *Queer Sinophone Cultures*. London: Routledge.

Chiang, H., and Wong, A. K. (eds.). (2020). *Keywords in Queer Sinophone Studies*. London: Routledge.

Chun, A. (2017). *Forget Chineseness: On the Geopolitics of Cultural Identification*. Albany: State University of New York Press.

Chun, A. (1996). Fuck Chineseness: On the ambiguities of ethnicity as culture as identity. *Boundary* 2(23), 111–138.

Chou, W.-S. (2000). *Tongzhi: Politics of Same-Sex Eroticism in Chinese Societies*. Binghamton, NY: Haworth Press.

Cui, L. (2023) 'Chinese academia wouldn't be tolerant of my research': Gay academics' concerns about conducting queer research in China. *Culture, Health and Sexuality* 25(4), 459–474. https://doi.org/10.1080/13691058.2022.2053750.

Cummings, J. (2022). *The Everyday Lives of Gay Men in Hainan Sociality, Space and Time*. London: Springer Nature.

Damm, J. (2005). Same sex desire and society in Taiwan, 1970–1987. *The China Quarterly* 181, 67–81.

Davies, B., and Harré, R. (1990). Positioning: The discursive production of selves. *Journal for the Theory of Social Behaviour* 20(1), 43–46. https://doi.org/10.1111/j.1468-5914.1990.tb00174.x.

Davis, D. S. (2014). Privatization of marriage in post-socialist China. *Modern China* 40(6), 551–577.

Davis, J. A., Smith, T. W. and Marsden, P. V. (2005). *General Social Surveys, 1972–2004* [Computer file]. 2nd ICPSR Version. Chicago, IL: National Opinion Research Center.

De Fina, A. (2013). Positioning level 3: Connecting local identity displays to macro social processes. *Narrative Inquiry* 23(1), 40–61.

De Fina, A., and Georgakopoulou, A. (2012). *Analyzing Narrative: Discourse and Sociolinguistic Perspectives*. Cambridge: Cambridge University Press.

De Fina, A., Schiffrin, D. and Bamberg, M. (eds.). (2006). *Discourse and Identity*. Cambridge: Cambridge University Press.

Decena, C. U. (2008). Tacit subjects. *GLQ: A Journal of Lesbian and Gay Studies* 14(2–3), 339–359.

Ding, R., and Song, L. (2023). Queer cultures in digital Asia|digital sexual publics: Understanding do-it-yourself gay porn and lived experiences of sexuality in China. *International Journal of Communication*, 17, 2463–2478.

Ellis-Petersen, H. (2016, 4 March). China bans depictions of gay people on television. *The Guardian*. www.theguardian.com/tv-and-radio/2016/mar/04/Chinabans-gay-people-television-clampdown-xi-jinping-censorship.

Engebretsen, E. L. (2014). *Queer Women in Urban China: An Ethnography*. London: Routledge.

Erni, J. N., and Spires, A. J. (2001). Glossy subjects: *GandL Magazine* and 'tonghzi' cultural visibility in Taiwan. *Sexualities* 4(1), 25–49.

Esarey, A., and Xiao, Q. (2011). Digital communication and political change in China. *International Journal of Communication* 5(22), 5298–5319.

Forrest, D. (1994). 'We're here, we're queer and we're not going shopping': Changing gay male identities in contemporary Britain. In A. Cornwall and N. Lindisfarne (eds.), *Dislocating Masculinity: Comparative Ethnographies* (pp. 97–110). London: Routledge.

Foucault, M. (1972). *The Archaeology of Knowledge: And the Discourse on Language* (A. M. Sheridan Smith, trans.). New York: Pantheon (original work published 1969).

Foucault, M. (1978). *The History of Sexuality* (Vols. 1 and 2). New York: Pantheon.

Freestone, P. (2023). Do 'Chinese gays come out?' A discursive-sociocultural approach to queer visibility amongst same-gender-attracted men in Chengdu, China. *Journal of Language and Sexuality* 12(2), 200–226. https://doi.org/10.1075/jls.21009.fre.

Freestone, P. (2024). The sociolinguistic navigation of sexual normativities among same-gender-attracted men in contemporary Chengdu, China. *Gender and Language* 18(1), 28–47.

Gee, J. P. (2014[1999]). *An Introduction to Discourse Analysis: Theory and Method*. 4th edition. London: Routledge.

Goffman, E. (1959). *The Presentation of Self in Everyday Life*. London: Harmondsworth.

Graff, A. (2010). Looking at pictures of gay men: Political uses of homophobia in contemporary Poland. *Public Culture* 22(3), 583–603.

Haas, B. (2017, 24 May). Taiwan's top court rules in favour of same-sex marriage. *The Guardian*. www.theguardian.com/world/2017/may/24/taiwans-topcourt-rules-in-favour-of-same-sex-marriage.

Hagström, L., and Nordin, A. H. (2020). China's 'politics of harmony' and the quest for soft power in international politics. *International Studies Review* 22(3), 507–525.

Hall, S., and Du Gay, P. (eds.) (1996). *Questions of Cultural Identity*. London: Sage.

Halverson, J. R., Goodall, H. L. and Corman, S. R. (2011). What is a master narrative? In *Master Narratives of Islamist Extremism* (pp. 11–26). New York: Palgrave Macmillan.

Hinsch, B. (1990). *Passions of the Cut Sleeve: The Male Homosexual Tradition in China*. Berkeley: University of California Press.

Ho, J. C.-J. (2008). Is global governance bad for East Asian queers? *GLQ: A Journal of Lesbian and Gay Studies* 14(4), 457–479.

Ho, L. W. W. (2010). *Gay and Lesbian Subculture in Urban China*. Abingdon: Routledge.

Ho, P. S. Y., Jackson, S., Cao, S., and Kwok, C. (2018). Sex with Chinese characteristics: Sexuality research in/on 21st-century China. *Journal of Sex Research* 55(4–5), 486–521.

Hsu, C.-Y., and Yen, C.-F. (2017). Taiwan: Pioneer of the health and well-being of sexual minorities in Asia. *Archives of Sexual Behavior* 46(6), 1577–1579.

Hu, X., and Wang, Y. (2013). LGB identity among young Chinese: The influence of traditional culture. *Journal of Homosexuality* 60(5), 667–684.

Huang, H. T.-M. (2011). *Queer Politics and Sexual Modernity in Taiwan*. Hong Kong: Hong Kong University Press.

Huang, S., and Brouwer, D. C. (2018). Coming out, coming home, coming with: Models of queer sexuality in contemporary China. *Journal of International and Intercultural Communication* 11(2), 97–116.

Jackson, P., Martin, F., McLelland, M. and Yue, A. (2008). *Asia PacifiQueer: Rethinking Genders and Sexualities*. Chicago: University of Illinois Press.

Jeffreys, E., and Yu, H. (2015). *Sex in China*. Cambridge: Polity Press.

Jones, L. (2018). 'I'm not proud, I'm just gay': Lesbian and gay youths' discursive negotiation of otherness. *Journal of Sociolinguistics* 22(1), 55–76.

Jones, R. H. (2016). *Spoken Discourse*. London: Bloomsbury.

Kam, L. Y. L. (2013). *Shanghai Lalas: Female Tongzhi Communities and Politics in Urban China*. Hong Kong: Hong Kong University Press.

King, G., Pan, J. and Roberts, M. E. (2013). How censorship in China allows government criticism but silences collective expression. *American Political Science Review* 107(2), 326–343.

Kong, T. S. K. (2011). *Chinese Male Homosexualities: Memba, Tongzhi and Golden Boy*. Oxford: Routledge.

Kong, T. S. K. (2016). The sexual in Chinese sociology: Homosexuality studies in contemporary China. *Sociological Review* 64(3), 495–514.

Kong, T. S. K. (2023). *Sexuality and the Rise of China: The Post-1990s Gay Generation in Hong Kong, Taiwan, and Mainland China*. Durham, NC: Duke University Press.

Kong, T. S. K. (2019). Transnational queer sociological analysis of sexual identity and civic-political activism in Hong Kong, Taiwan and mainland China. *British Journal of Sociology* 70(5): 1904–1925. https://doi.org/10.1111/1468-4446.12697.

Landry, R., and Bourhis, R. Y. (1997). Linguistic landscape and ethnolinguistic vitality: An empirical study. *Journal of Language and Social Psychology*, 16(1), 23–49.

Le Page, R., and Tabouret-Keller, A. (1985). *Acts of Identity: Creole-based Approaches to Language and Ethnicity*. Cambridge: Cambridge University Press.

Lee, P. H. (2016). LGBT rights versus Asian values: De/re-constructing the universality of human rights. *International Journal of Human Rights* 20(7), 978–992.

Lee, P. H. (2017). Queer activism in Taiwan: An emergent rainbow coalition from the assemblage perspective. *Sociological Review*, 65(4), 682–698.

Li, C. (2006). The Confucian ideal of harmony. *Philosophy East and West* 56(4), 583–603. www.jstor.org/stable/4488054.

Li, C. (2013). *The Confucian Philosophy of Harmony*. London: Routledge.

Li, Y. [Yinhe] (1998). *Tongxinglian yawenhua* [*The Subculture of Homosexuality*]. Beijing: Jinri Zhongguo Chubanshe.

Li, Y. [Yinhe], and Wang, X. (1992). *Tamen de shijie: Zhongguo nan tongxinglian qunluo toushi* [*Their World: Looking into the Male Homosexual Community in China*]. Hong Kong: Cosmos Books.

Liu, P. (2007). Queer Marxism in Taiwan. *Inter-Asia Cultural Studies*, 8(4), 517–539.

Liu, P. (2015). *Queer Marxism in Two Chinas*. Durham, NC: Duke University Press.

Liu, P. (2010). Why does queer theory need China? *Positions: East Asia Cultures Critique* 18(2), 291–320.

Liu, P., and Rofel, L. (2010). Beyond the strai(gh)ts: Transnationalism and queer Chinese politics. *Positions: East Asia Cultures Critique* 18(2), 281–289.

Liu, X. (2021). Homonationalist and homocolonialist discourses in Hong Kong's anti-extradition protests: Online evaluations and representations of LGBT rights. *Discourse, Context and Media* 40, 100465.

Martin, F. (2003). *Situating Sexualities: Queer Representation in Taiwanese Fiction, Film and Public Culture*. Hong Kong: Hong Kong University Press.

Martin, F. (2014). Transnational queer Sinophone cultures. In M. McLelland and V. Mackie (eds.), *The Routledge Handbook of Sexuality Studies in East Asia* (pp. 35–48). Abingdon: Routledge.

Miller, C. J. (2023). *Inside the Circle: Queer Culture and Activism in Northwest China*. New Brunswick, NJ: Rutgers University Press.

Motschenbacher, H. (2020). Coming out and normative shifts: Investigating usage patterns of gay and homosexual in a corpus of news reports on Ricky Martin. *Sociolinguistic Studies* 14(1–2), 61–84.

Motschenbacher, H. (2021). Language and sexuality studies today: Why 'homosexual' is a bad word and why 'queer linguist' is not an identity. *Journal of Language and Sexuality* 10(1), 25–36.

Motschenbacher, H. (2011). Taking queer linguistics further: Sociolinguistics and critical heteronormativity research. *International Journal of the Sociology of Language* 212, 149–179.

Motschenbacher, H., and Stegu, M. (2013). Queer linguistic approaches to discourse. *Discourse and Society* 24(5), 519–535.

National Election Study (2004). *The 2004 National Election Study* [Computer file]. Ann Arbor: Center for Political Studies, University of Michigan.

Oswin, N. (2006). Decentering queer globalization: Diffusion and the 'global gay'. *Environment and Planning D: Society and Space*, 24(5), 777–790.

Rofel, L. (2007). *Desiring China: Experiments in Neoliberalism, Sexuality, and Public Culture*. Durham, NC: Duke University Press.

Roseneil, S., and Stoilova, M. (2016 [2011]). Heteronormativity, intimate citizenship and the regulation of same-sex sexualities in Bulgaria. In R. Kulpa and J. Mizielińska (eds.), *De-centring Western Sexualities: Central and Eastern European Perspectives* (pp. 167–190). Abingdon: Routledge.

Russell, E. L. (2021). *Alpha Masculinity: Hegemony in Language and Discourse*. Palgrave Macmillan.

Russell, S. T., Clarke, T. J. and Clary, J. (2009). Are teens 'post-gay'? Contemporary adolescents' sexual identity labels. *Journal of Youth and Adolescence*, 38, 884–890.

Savin-Williams, R. C. (2005). *The New Gay Teenager*. Cambridge, MA: Harvard University Press.

Scollon, R., Scollon, S. W. and Jones, R. H. (2012). *Intercultural Communication: A Discourse Approach* (3rd ed.). Oxford: John Wiley and Sons.

Shaw, G., and Zhang, X. (2018). Cyberspace and gay rights in a digital China: Queer documentary filmmaking under state censorship. *China Information* 32(2), 270–292.

Shih, S. M. (2007). *Visuality and Identity: Sinophone Articulations across the Pacific*. Berkeley: University of California Press.

Song, L. (2021). *Queering Chinese Kinship: Queer Public Culture in Globalizing China*. Hong Kong: Hong Kong University Press.

Sunderland, J. (2004). *Gendered Discourses*. Basingstoke: Palgrave Macmillan.

Tamney, J. B., and Chiang, L. H.-L. (2002). *Modernization, Globalization, and Confucianism in Chinese Societies*. Westport, CT: Praeger.

Tan, C. K. (2001). Transcending sexual nationalism and colonialism: Cultural hybridisation as process of sexual politics in '90s Taiwan. In J. C. Hawley (ed.), *Postcolonial, Queer: Theoretical Intersections* (pp. 123–138). New York: State University of New York Press.

Tudor, M. (2018). *Desire Lines: Towards a Queer Digital Media Phenomenology*. Stockholm: Södertörns högskola.

United Nations Development Programme (UNDP) and United States Agency for International Development (USAID) (2014). *Being LGBT in Asia: China Country Report*. Bangkok: United Nations Development Programme.

Wang, F. T. Y., Bih, H.-D. and Brennan, D. J. (2009). Have they really come out? Gay men and their parents in Taiwan. *Culture, Health and Sexuality*, 11(3), 285–296.

Wang, G., and Ma, X. (2020). Representations of LGBTQ+ issues in China in its official English-language media: A corpus-assisted critical discourse study. *Critical Discourse Studies* 18(3), 1–19.

Wei, W. (2018). The normalization project: The progress and limitations of promoting LGBTQ research and teaching in mainland China. *Journal of Homosexuality* 67(3), 335–345.

Wei, W. (2021). Queering the rise of China: Gay parenthood, transnational ARTs, and dislocated reproductive rights. *Feminist Studies* 47(2), 312–340.

Wei, W. (2007). 'Wandering men' no longer wander around: The production and transformation of local homosexual identities in contemporary Chengdu, China. *Inter-Asia Cultural Studies* 8(4), 572–588.

Whyte, M. K. (1997). The fate of filial obligations in urban China. *China Journal*, 38, 1–31.

Wong, A. D. (2005b). Language, cultural authenticity, and the *tongzhi* movement. In S. Finch, T. Ikeda, M. Shetty, and C. Sunakawa (eds.), *Texas Linguistic Forum* (Vol. 48). Proceedings of the Twelfth Annual Symposium about Language and Society, held at University of Texas, Austin, 2004, April 16–18 (pp. 209–215). Austin: University of Texas Press.

Wong, A. D. (2008a). On the actuation of semantic change: The case of *tongzhi*. *Language Sciences* 30(4), 423–449.

Wong, A. D. (2005a). The reappropriation of *tongzhi*. *Language in Society* 34(5), 763–793.

Wong, A. D. (2008b). The trouble with *tongzhi*: The politics of labelling among gay and lesbian Hongkongers. *Pragmatics* 18(2), 277–301.

Xie, Y., and Peng, M. (2018). Attitudes toward homosexuality in China: Exploring the effects of religion, modernizing factors, and traditional culture. *Journal of Homosexuality* 65(13), 1758–1787.

Yan, A. (2016, 23 February) Chinese web drama pulled from internet, sparking backlash. *South China Morning Post*. Retrieved from www.scmp.com/news/China/society/article/1915975/chinese-gay-drama-pulledinternet-sparking-backlash.

Yang, Y. (2019). Bargaining with the state: The empowerment of Chinese sexual minorities/LGBT in the social media era. *Journal of Contemporary China* 28(118), 662–677.

Yuen, S. (2015). Friend or foe? The diminishing space of China's civil society. *China Perspectives*, 3, 51–56.

Zhang, B. (1994). *Tongxing'ai*. Jinan: Shandong Science and Technology Press.

Zhang, B., and Chu, Q. (2005). MSM and HIV/AIDS in China. *Cell Research* 15(11), 858–864.

Zhang, B., Li, X., Chu, Q. et al. (2008). A survey of HIV/AIDS related behaviors among 2250 MSM in nine major cities of China. *Chinese Journal of AIDS & STD* 14(6), 541–547.

Zheng, T. (2015). Tongzhi *Living: Men Attracted to Men in Postsocialist China*. Minneapolis: University of Minnesota Press.

Zhou, T. (2018). Jack'd, Douban Group, and Feizan.com: The impact of cyberqueer technopractice on the Chinese gay male experience. In J. T. Grider and D. van Reenen (eds.), *Exploring Erotic Encounters* (pp. 27–43). At the Interface/Probing the Boundaries 93. London: Brill.

Zhou, Z. B. (2022). 'Besides *tongzhi*: Tactics for constructing and communicating sexual identities in China.' *Journal of Linguistic Anthropology* 32(2), 282–300.

*Thanks to Mike Baynham, Niko Besnier, Mie Hiramoto,
Rodney Jones, Brian King, James Simpson, Helen Sauntson
and all my Sinophone friends for their ideas . . .
. . . and to Edison Tam for unconditional support and love.*

Cambridge Elements

Language, Gender and Sexuality

Helen Sauntson
York St John University

Helen Sauntson is Professor of English Language and Linguistics at York St John University, UK. Her research areas are language in education and language, gender and sexuality. She is co-editor of *The Palgrave Studies in Language, Gender and Sexuality* book series, and she sits on the editorial boards of the journals *Gender and Language* and the *Journal of Language and Sexuality*. Within her institution, Helen is Director of the Centre for Language and Social Justice Research.

Holly R. Cashman
University of New Hampshire

Holly R. Cashman is Professor of Spanish at University of New Hampshire (USA), core faculty in Women's and Gender Studies, and coordinator of Queer Studies. She is past president of the International Gender and Language Association (IGALA) and of the executive board of the Association of Language Departments (ALD) of the Modern Languages Association. Her research interests include queer(ing) multilingualism and language, gender, and sexuality.

Editorial Board
Lilian Lem Atanga, *The University of Bamenda*
Eva Nossem, *Saarland University*
Joshua M. Paiz, *The George Washington University*
M. Agnes Kang, *University of Hong Kong*

About the Series
Cambridge Elements in Language, Gender and Sexuality highlights the role of language in understanding issues, identities and relationships in relation to multiple genders and sexualities. The series provides a comprehensive home for key topics in the field which readers can consult for up-to-date coverage and the latest developments.

Cambridge Elements

Language, Gender and Sexuality

Elements in the Series

The Language of Gender-Based Separatism
Veronika Koller, Alexandra Krendel and Jessica Aiston

Queering Sexual Health Translation Pedagogy
Piero Toto

Legal Categorization of "Transgender": An Analysis of Statutory Interpretation of "Sex", "Man", and "Woman" in Transgender Jurisprudence
Kimberly Tao

LGBTQ+ and Feminist Digital Activism: A Linguistic Perspective
Angela Zottola

Feminism, Corpus-assisted Research and Language Inclusivity
Federica Formato

Queering Language Revitalisation: Navigating Identity and Inclusion among Queer Speakers of Minority Languages
John Walsh, Michael Hornsby, Eva J. Daussà, Renée Pera-Ros, Samuel Parker, Jonathan Morris and Holly R. Cashman

Pride in Asia: Negotiating Ideologies, Localness, and Alternative Futures
Benedict J. L. Rowlett, Pavadee Saisuwan, Christian Go,
Li-Chi Chen and Mie Hiramoto

Language, Gender and Pregnancy Loss
Beth Malory

Discourse and Queer Sinophone Male Identities: A Western Immigrant Perspective
Phil Freestone

A full series listing is available at: www.cambridge.org/ELGS

Printed by Integrated Books International,
United States of America